Programming Problems

A Primer for The Technical Interview

Volume II: Advanced Algorithms

Bradley GREEN
ALGORITHMIST@HOTMAIL.COM
Spring, 2013

Preface

This book is the study guide I wish I had when preparing for my first programming interview.

After graduation I was unprepared for the gauntlet of the technical interview. At that time, in quick succession IBM, Intel, and Microsoft interviewed me. Microsoft was far and away the most difficult interview, spanning 2 days and 14 total interviews. We covered everything; makefiles and build environments, digital circuits, C/C++ language specifications, and algorithms. Luckily, in the end everything worked out fine. I evaluated my offers, and moved to Redmond, Washington to begin my career in high tech. However, I still wish I knew what I was getting myself into before I had my first tech interview.

In tech, nothing stays very stable for long. Projects change and company wide reorganizations happen without notice. Its not a well kept secret, but at Microsoft internal transfers require a full technical interview. Now and again there are exceptions, for instance if you are well known in the area or if you are re-organized into a different division. But for the most part you have a full interview, including external resume submission, pre-interview screening, and the grueling day of testing.

So soon into the new millennium, I began interviewing for my second position. Since that time I've interviewed many more times at Microsoft, Google, Facebook, and a host of other high tech companies. I'm lucky to have always passed the interviews, and have spent time at a number of great companies.

During all this I've conducted over a hundred interviews and discussed many more in interview loops and hiring committees. Some years ago I began saving notes for when I prepare to give interviews. These became organized into a large collection of programming problems. At some point a friend mentioned that it would be worthwhile to write these down, and from that suggestion has come this book.

This book is meant as a refresher for seasoned engineers and a handbook for first candidates; it is not a textbook or a scientific volume. I considered adding sections with problems at the end of each chapter, but I believe that without complete answers this text loses its focus as a handbook. In further editions the references made in the text will be properly compiled into a bibliography, but for the moment I beg your forgiveness for not knowing where many of the techniques used herein were first discovered. And finally, although I've done my best to guarantee the code presented compiles with `gcc4.7` and works on basic test cases, there are not many references or mathematical proofs in the first edition of this book.

0.1   Structure of the book

There are three main areas that I hope to cover in this work: data structures, searching and sorting, and advanced algorithms. The later section of the text is broken up into algorithms on strings, numbers, and sequences. As the scope of this work grew, it became clear that the work should be divided into two volumes. The first volume provides a discussion of programming problems covering elementary data structures, abstract data types, searching and sorting. The second volume covers advanced programming problems such as spatial partitioning, substring searching, parsing, and sampling.

The chapter structure is the same within both volumes. Each chapter is a self-contained study guide on a specific topic. I attempted to frame it so that complexity increases throughout the chapter. The introductory material should be simply refresher for anyone in the industry; middle sections contain interesting problems and revisions, and the finale an interesting and complex problem. I hope that these problems give the reader some pleasure in thinking about before continuing on to the discussion of the answer.

0.2   Programming in C/C++

`C/C++` has long been the standard for advanced programming. If you want to work alongside the best in our field you should take the time to familiarize yourself with this language at least to the level of reading comprehension. And to be clear, if you want to work at a company such as Apple, Facebook, Google, or Microsoft you are handicapping yourself and your future if you do not know C/C++.

C/C++ is the lingua franca of interviewing; nearly all interviewers know it and nearly all candidates are expected to be able to read it. But there are many reasons aside from just the fact that most of the interviewers at those companies are familiar with C/C++. For one, C/C++ hides very little. While this makes writing code more verbose, it allows everyone to know what you are trying to demonstrate. And being able to clearly demonstrate what you know is what an interview is all about.

The coding style used here loosely follows the style guidelines published by Google. I find the format they have come to agree upon and evangelize to favor readability over conciseness. In the listings most coding will be verbose in many areas, aside from some pointer arithmetic and parameter variable reuse.

I attempt to stay close to the C roots of the C++ language at the expense of class definitions, templates and generic solutions. This is done so as to demonstrate the algorithms as clearly as possible. The benefits of templates and container classes are not lost to me, and I use them in everyday coding. But they add complexity to the code listings that does not justify their weight. For that reason nearly all the value data types will simply be int. It should be clear that for almost everywhere they are used that a template version of the function or a proper data structure container could be substituted.

I did not want to write this text in ANSI C, so to avoid many lines of text due to memory management I will use the STL containers *queue*, *stack*, and *vector*, freely. But there will be some pointer arithmetic and in fact an entire section on bit twiddling in the second volume.

Near the end of writing the first draft, I decided to incorporate C++11. The revision vastly improves readability and conciseness. The use of auto allows the reader to focus on the variable use and not the variable declaration. I call elements of type std::function functionals. The use of functionals keeps algorithms self-contained instead of spread out amongst many functions. I hope this change benefits the reader as much as it did the writer.

0.3   Acknowledgements

I want to thank L.A.G. for her support and endearing love, and always being there by my side. I also want to thank T.G. for always being there to offer a short diversion to writing, and to my parents R.G. and K.G., for without them I would have never gotten this far.

I also want to thank J. Melvin for a thorough reading, and his helpful comments. The editors of Wikipedia made research extremely efficient, and there is not enough that I can do to thank them for their contribution. And finally, I am grateful to to E.M.H. for suggesting this book and her reminder that it should have been completed long ago.

0.4   A last word

In further editions, I hope to make this resemble a proper scientific text. That will require thorough references and proper arguments instead of oblique mentions and assertions of fact. To that end, I am happy to receive your corrections, references, and suggestions regarding any of the material in here at `algorithmist@hotmail.com`.

Preface To The Second Volume

The second volume of Programming Problems has taken me longer to complete than originally promised. The date of late 2012 was a date I believed could be accomplished. However with the growth of my family and transitions at work, time moved faster than I ever thought it could.

I want to thank the many readers of the first volume for your comments and recommendations. I really enjoyed hearing from you, and hope I can continue my side of the dialog going forward.

Contents

Listings

To Ada, on her first birthday.

Chapter 1

Advanced Algorithms

A digest of advanced algorithms is hard to qualify. Topics that were advanced in the field many years ago may be taught at an elementary level today. What is advanced for the novice may be obvious to the expert. Across domains, an advanced technique in one specialization may be a simple application of the tools of another. The specification of being advanced is hence somewhat arbitrary, but we will try to be consistent in its application.

1.1 What comes next

In the first volume, we explored elementary abstract data structures and simple algorithmic applications of them to programming problems. We visited elementary algorithms that employed these data structures, such as searching, selection, and sorting. These were elementary not because they were simple but because of the generality of their application. We now shift our focus to specialized data structures used to solve specialized problem. It is not specialization that makes an algorithm advanced, but instead is the amount of information required to develop and understand the algorithm. And that information requirement makes advanced algorithms interesting.

There is a difference between elementary algorithms and naive algorithms. An elementary algorithm such as binary search or merge sort can be employed in almost universally. A naive algorithm may solve a specialized problem, but it is a solution to that uses the first workable approach without regard to time or space. In doing so it employs elementary algorithms mechanically. However with only a little finesse, a much better solution can often be developed that provides a much better solution. Quantitatively, a better solution is one that has reduced internal complexity, shorter computation complexity, or leverages insights developed in similar problems.

When choosing advanced algorithms for this volume, I have attempted to present interesting algorithms as well as deep algorithms.

Interesting algorithms demonstrate neat tricks and clever transforms. A neat trick is a subroutine that often takes a step towards the solution in an unexpected way. We will begin with bit twiddling, and the trick of clearing the last bit leads to an efficient mechanism for finding discrete logarithms. We will explore how clever use of the greedy algorithm can affect paragraph justification, and see how small calculations can be used to correctly sample from streaming data.

A deep algorithm uncovers connections between different problem domains. A deep algorithm can also demonstrate the use of a new technique. For instance the Knuth-Morris-Pratt string matching algorithm demonstrates how to apply a finite state machine to pattern matching. For instance, the Newton's method is deep because it demonstrates how calculus can be used to solve equations without requiring a closed form solution. Bentley's k-d tree is deep because it shows how to navigate space in an efficient pattern to affect multi-dimensional search.

I hope you find the selection of programming problems here entertaining and enlightening.

1.2   Learning algorithms

Algorithms are recipes for solutions. They require ingredients as input, proper mixture of calculations, space to work and time to develop. The problem may be how to find a needle in a haystack of unordered data. The problem may be how to store data so that it is easily retrieved. Or the problem may be how to identify a specific item from a stream of items. An algorithm describes the steps needed to move from statement to solution.

Computer science is generally taught in a progression. A course of study starts with data structures and progresses towards elementary algorithms. A language is taught in tandem with these topics, but the language is ancillary. The focus then shifts to the basics of programming languages, operating systems, and networking. Finally, the student finds himself branching into specialized topics such as distributed computing, computer vision, and machine learning. However, the study of algorithms does not need to follow this progression. While the applications may be motivating, the development and theory of algorithms is itself rewarding.

A solution to a programming problem can be understood at many levels. These volumes focus on providing understanding in two paths. Often we develop a solution from a naive to an optimal approach. And often we develop a technique in application to many related problems. The first method is demonstrated in our discussion of calculating Fibonacci numbers. We produce and discuss many different methods to tackle the same problem but all ultimately find the same solution. The second method is demonstrated in our discussions of recursion and dynamic programming.

Computer science is mathematical in nature and requires proof of correctness of algorithms. Generally, this follows the pattern of maintaining an invariant such that if no other action is possible then the solution is obvious. Items are sorted, a minimum is found, the optimal is retrieved. In this volume, we do not take a mathematical approach to explaining algorithms, although it is extremely important to do so. I urge the reader to explore beyond the confines presented here.

For the problems here, pause after the problem statement. Endeavor to follow the same procedure that is used in answering interview questions. Restate the problem in your own words, and develop a better understanding of the problem through examples. Attempt to write out some test cases, paying special attention to the boundary cases. Then think of the simplest solution available for a typical instance and outline the recipe. Only then is it time to read the solution provided in the text.

The listings provided in the text are implementations of algorithms. When you are reading an them, keep in mind that the objective is to understand the algorithm and not the implementation. The algorithm can be understood from a high level and low-level perspective. From a high level understand the main objective of the outer loops, if there is a helper function or utility function what is its purpose in terms of input and output. It is useful to give a name these substructures that describes their purpose. Understand first how the machinery is translating the input to the output. Discover how is each operation getting closer to the solution.

Once the high level picture is clear, set to work understanding the algorithm at a low level. Understand the reason behind the choice of data structure, and discover when or why the input is modified. Determine the objective of every temporary value and small grouping of lines of code. Graph the conditional branching and determine why such a division was made.

Being able to solve problems quickly and efficient is the result of experience. Throughout our education in algorithms, we see the same tricks repeatedly. The same way calculus students see the same derivations repeatedly. What is important is that these tools are recognized, internalized, and their application to programming problems becomes habit. For instance, pre-sorting, using a heap to find a minimum, using a stack to keep state, using queues to order elements by their time of discovery are applied by habit when an engineer because to tackle a new problem.

This top down method for learning algorithms lends itself to the process of solving new programming problems. A thorough understanding of the difficulties comes first. The design an algorithm follows from this. Algorithms are designed from the top down, and implemented from the bottom up. We first ask how is it possible to make a single step toward the solution? Would sorting help? Would partitioning help? What techniques could modify the data into sub problems that are more easily tackled? Is recursion a viable method? Should I memoize or use tail recursive. Once these questions are answered it is time to begin coding.

There is an art to the practice of algorithm design. The more a problem can be broken down in to smaller sub problems the easier it is to design a solution. Mastery of this art only comes from practice. There are many of ways to practice. The best is to program every day. This does not require taking on the challenges of redesigning operating system file handling or writing a word processor. There are plenty of opportunities to use a computer to solve questions that come up routinely. For instance if you want to know the mean value of a set of numbers, if you want to understand how a random process behaves, if you want to find a route through a maze or the solution to a crossword puzzle. More importantly there is practice in improvement. Optimal algorithms rarely present themselves fully formed. They are improved by iteration and refinement. Every solution has presents an opportunity for improvement. Embrace these opportunities.

Reading algorithms is a starting point, but it is not enough in itself. Practice is required for mastery. Practice can come from typing in code from computing magazines and reference books. Practice can come from reading periodic articles and specialized text. But the best practice is to code at every opportunity.

Now lets get on with it.

Chapter 2

Bit Twiddling

Backend engineers enjoy when they can find reason to program close to the metal. Saving 8 bytes by ridding our code of a superfluous variable is a reason for celebration. Finding a trick to optimize out an unnecessary instruction makes the day a little better.

Still one of the most frustrating types of questions are those which ask you to forgo higher level data structures and complex instructions and revert to bit twiddling and logical operations. Whether it is saving memory by using a bit array, optimizing arithmetic by bit shifting or arithmetic tricks, it is worthwhile to know these techniques.

In this chapter we will cover many techniques dealing with bit twiddling. After a brief review of bit operations in C++, we solve the power of two decision problem. We then look at counting bits and bit folding. We conclude this section by implementing multiplication and division using only bitwise operations.

2.1 Overview

We provide a brief discussion of the support for bit operations, bit fields, and bit arrays in C++.

The bit operations in C++ are listed in the following table. There is a single unary operator and five binary operators. The not unary operator flips the value of every bit in a variable. The binary operators are and, or, and xor perform logical operations on the corresponding bits of the operands. The final binary operators are the left and right shift operators, which respectively perform multiplication and division by 2 on the binary representation of a value. These should be familiar to the reader.

Bitwise Operator	Syntax	Example
NOT	$\sim x$	$\sim 0011 \to 1100$
AND	$x \& y$	$0011 \& 1001 \to 0001$
OR	$x \vert y$	$0011 \vert 1001 \to 1011$
XOR	$x \char`^ y$	$0011 \char`^ 1001 \to 1010$
Left Shift	$x \ll y$	$0011 \ll 1 \to 0110$
Right Shift	$x \gg y$	$0011 \gg 1 \to 0001$

C++ also supports the bit field structure. The structure allows a programmer to divide up an integer into named blocks of bits. The block size can be specified in the declaration of the bit field. A typical definition looks similar to below.

Listing 2.1: Defining a Bit Field

```
1  struct bitfield {
2    unsigned one  : 1;
3    unsigned two  : 2;
4    unsigned      : 2;
5    unsigned three: 3;
6  };
```

Here, the `two` subfield is 2 bits in length, and is separated from the `three` subfield by padding of 2 bits. Declaring and instance of this structure and accessing a field is straightforward.

Listing 2.2: Declaring and Accessing A Bit Field

```
1  bitfield a;
2  a.two = 1;
```

The `stl std::bitset` provides support for accessing a continuous array of bits as a vector. A `bitset` can be thought of as a bit field of single elements accessed by index instead of by name. The length of a bitset array is defined at compile time by a template parameter. The individual bits of a bitset can be accessed by operator[].

Listing 2.3: Declaring and Accessing the stl Bitset

```
1  std::bitset<64> bits64;
2  bits64[1] = 1;
3  bits64[63] = 0;
```

The stl std::vector container has a specialization for dynamically sized bit arrays. This specialization can be accessed by declaring the variable of type std::vector<bool>. This specialization provides more flexibility than a biset in that it can be resized. It also provides iterators to the underlying data. However it does not support many binary operations such as bitwise and, or, and not.

In the sequel, our bit operations can be understood by doing without these containers. For that reason we will often use unsigned types as bit arrays instead of these constructs.

2.2 Power of two

We begin with a progression of solutions to the problem of deciding whether or not a value is a power of two. In a binary representation, a value is a power of two when exactly a single bit is set. There is a single bit of value 1, and all other bits have value 0. So a count of the number of set bits will solve the problem. There are two common iterative solutions for this problem.

The first is by iterating through all bits and counting the set bits. Each bit is visited by shifting the right and masking the last bit. In a 32-bit integer, we need to iterate that many times.

Listing 2.4: Power of Two by Iterating

```
1  bool power_of_two(unsigned x) {
2    auto ones_count = 0;
3    for (auto index = 0; index < 32; ++index) {
4      if (0x1 & x) ++ones_count;
5      x = x >> 1;
6    }
7    return ones_count == 1;
8  }
```

The second is by enumerating all powers of two, and checking each in turn against the operand. Here, instead of masking a single bit we check equality between a known power of two and the given value. We start with the value 1 and iteratively shift it left.

Listing 2.5: Power of Two by Shifting

```
1  bool power_of_two(unsigned x) {
2    auto y = 0x1;
3    while (0 != y) {
4      if (x == y) return true;
5      y = y << 1;
6    }
7    return false;
8  }
```

Both of these are inefficient in that they can check all of the locations in the worst case.

There is a standard one-line trick to this problem that gives a lot of insight into bit operations. The trick is to clear the least significant bit of the value test for zero.

Listing 2.6: Power of Two

```
1  bool power_of_two(unsigned x) {
2    if (!x) return false;
3    return 0 == (x & (x-1));
4  }
```

When 1 is subtracted from a number, the least significant bit is cleared and all preceding unset bits are set. For instance $0100 - 0001 = 0011$. So in $x - 1$ we know that the least significant bit of x is not set, all proceeding bits are set. So if there is any other bit set, then that bit will be set in $x \& (x - 1)$. Note we check if x equals 0 first, otherwise the test fails with underflow.

2.3 Lowest order bit

Clearing the least significant bit is a standard bit twiddling trick, and deserves to be named.

Listing 2.7: Clear the Least Significant Bit

```
1  unsigned clear_last_bit(unsigned x) {
2    return x & (x - 1);
3  }
```

This one liner has many other applications. Suppose we want to identify and isolate the least significant set bit. To do so we can negate the value with the lowest set bit, and & the original value with that value.

Listing 2.8: Isolate the Least Significant Bit

```
1  unsigned lowest_set_bit(unsigned x) {
2    return x & ~(x-1);
3  }
```

This can be used in efficient counting of set bits.

Consider another implementation of counting the number of set bits. Below we iterate using indexing of a bit array.

Listing 2.9: Count Set Bits Iteratively

```
1  unsigned count_bits_set(unsigned x) {
2    unsigned count = 0;
3    for (int index = 0; index < 32; ++index) {
4      if (x & (0x1 << index)) ++count;
5    }
6    return count;
7  }
```

Some inefficiency is in this problem because we test bit locations whence there is an unset bit. But by clearing the last bit instead of iterating, the same result can be achieved with only has one comparison per set bit. We gain efficiency, since on average we will have half as many comparisons.

Listing 2.10: Count Set Bits

```
1  unsigned count_bits_set(unsigned x) {
2    unsigned count = 0;
3    while (x) {
4      x = clear_last_bit(x);
5      ++count;
6    }
7    return count;
8  }    .
```

2.4   Folding over

Folding a value over itself another standard bit twiddling trick. In a sense, folding is the opposite of clearing the last bit. The result of folding is setting all bits after the most significant. The operation is defined below for 32 bit integers.

Listing 2.11: Folding Over

```
1  unsigned fold_over(unsigned x) {
2      x |= (x >> 1);
3      x |= (x >> 2);
4      x |= (x >> 4);
5      x |= (x >> 8);
6      x |= (x >> 16);
7      return x;
8  }
```

Understand what this code is achieving. In the first operation, every bit sets the bit to its immediately right. In the next, every bit sets the bit two over, then the next sets the bit four away, etc. If the top bit is initially set, the first iteration sets two bits. The second sets four bits, and this continues until the last operation successfully sets all bits.

Our first application of folding is to isolate the highest set bit. This is done by masking off all but the most significant bit after folding.

Listing 2.12: Isolate the Highest Set Bit

```
1  unsigned int highest_set_bit(unsigned int x) {
2      x = fold_over(x);
3      return (x & ~(x >> 1));
4  }
```

This is the opposite of clearing the lowest set bit.

Let us put this to use. The position of the most significant bit gives the log of the power of two. Note that after folding, adding one sets the next most significant bit and clears all the other bits. So counting the position of the most significant bit we calculate the log rounded up to the next integer. Note though what happens when a value is a power of two, we are rounding up when we should not. So we normalize the value by first subtracting one to avoid this edge case.

Listing 2.13: Calculate $\log_2 x$

```
1  unsigned int log_x(unsigned int x) {
2     x = x - 1;
3     x = fold_over(x);
4     x = x + 1;
5     for (auto index = 0; index < 32; ++index) {
6        if (x == (0x1 << index)) return index;
7     }
8     return 0;
9  }
```

Another application of folding is finding the next power of two greater than a value. This is as simple as removing the normalizer from the log function above.

Listing 2.14: Find the Next Highest Power of Two

```
1  unsigned next_power_of_two(unsigned x) {
2     x = fold_over(x);
3     return x+1;
4  }
```

2.5   Reverse a bit vector

A modification of the successive shifting used in folding can be used to reverse the bits of an unsigned integer in a clever way. The idea is to swap the top and bottom halves of an integer, then recursively swap the top and bottom halves of the swapped halves until neighbors are swapped. Once neighbors are swapped, the bits of the integer have been reversed.

```
   Listing 2.15: Reverse Bits
1  unsigned reverse_bits(unsigned x) {
2    x = ((x & 0xffff0000) >> 16) |
3          ((x & 0x0000ffff) << 16);
4    x = ((x & 0xff00ff00) >> 8) |
5          ((x & 0x00ff00ff) << 8);
6    x = ((x & 0xf0f0f0f0) >> 4) |
7          ((x & 0x0f0f0f0f) << 4);
8    x = ((x & 0xcccccccc) >> 2) |
9          ((x & 0x33333333) << 2);
10   x = ((x & 0xaaaaaaaa) >> 1) |
11         ((x & 0x55555555) << 1);
12   return x;
13 }
```

Notice that the first constants are values where every other group of 16 bits is set. In the second, every other group of 8 bits are set. Then every other group of 4 bits, next every other couple, and finally every other bit.

While there is some complexity to the solution, note that the iterative solution requires a linear number of bitwise swaps. This implementation is taking time logarithmic in the length of the input, a significant increase.

2.6 Bitwise arithmetic

A common question is to implement arithmetic operations without the use of their operations. In this section, we will see how bit operations can be used to solve these questions efficiently for multiplication and division.

2.6.1 Bitwise multiplication

Consider implementing multiplication of integers without using the operator *. Recall when multiplying by hand, we iteratively multiply the first argument by each digit in the second. The result within an iteration is shifted left according to the position of the second digit, and then the result is added to a running total. With bits, we need only shift and add if the bit being considered is set.

Listing 2.16: Bitwise Multiplication

```
1  int multiply(int x, int y) {
2      int product = 0;
3      while (y) {
4          product += x << log_x(lowest_set_bit(y));
5          y = clear_last_bit(y);
6      }
7      return product;
8  }
```

It is interesting to note that the algorithm above works for negative operands. The standard binary representation of negative numbers is the twos-complement of the positive representation. To form the twos-complement of a value x, we compute $x+1$. In this representation there is no negative zero. A property of the twos-complement is that multiplication can be done bitwise without first representing each value as a positive integer.

2.6.2   Bitwise division

Lastly, we look at the more difficult question of implementing integer division without using either the division or modulus operations.

The idea is to understand how long division operates, and reproduce the algorithm with bit operations. In long division, to form a remainder we repeatedly shift and append the next digit of the numerator. If the denominator is smaller than the remainder, we subtract the integer multiple of the division from remainder, save this as the next digit of the quotient, and iterate. In binary, the simplification is that either the divisor goes into the remainder once or not at all. So we have a short inner loop.

However, long division on bits needs to take care to preserve sign. The reason for this is that we are comparing whether or not a positive remainder is larger than a positive denominator. For this reason, we first normalize the parameters to positive integers and then proceed. The sign is remedied before returning the result. But the process adds a preamble to our solution.

Listing 2.17: Bitwise Long Division

```
1  int divide(int x, int y) {
2    auto x_neg = x < 0;
3    auto y_neg = y < 0;
4    if (x_neg) x = ~x + 1;
5    if (y_neg) y = ~y + 1;
6    unsigned remainder = 0;
7    unsigned quotient = 0;
8    for (auto i = 32; i > 0; --i) {
9      quotient <<= 1;
10     remainder = (remainder << 1)
11                 + (0 != (x & (1 << (i-1)))));
12     if (remainder >= y)  {
13       quotient |= 1;
14       remainder = remainder - y;
15     }
16   }
17   if (x_neg != y_neg) quotient = ~quotient + 1;
18   return quotient;
19 }
```

It is worthwhile to spend a few moments to recognize that the code above is affecting long division. We keep a remainder throughout all iterations. In each iteration, we consider the next bit of the numerator. We begin by shifting the remainder to the left and appending this bit to the value. We then set the next bit of the quotient if and only if the denominator is larger than the remainder. If a bit is set, the denominator is subtracted from the remainder and we iterate.

Chapter 3

Big Integer Arithmetic

3.1 Big integer arithmetic

At the other end of the spectrum from bits are arbitrary precision integers. Often these are referred to as big num or `bigints`. Although the arithmetic between bits and `bigints` is similar, there are some challenges unique to variable sized operators.

In this chapter we will look at some common problems involving the use of big integer arithmetic. We first implement addition of arbitrary precision integers. Next we discuss negation and addition of signed big integers. Finally, we conclude with a look at multiplication of big integers.

3.2 Definition

A `bigint` is a representation of an integer value that allows for an unbounded number of digits. This is often accomplished by representing a big integer as an `unsigned char` vector.

Listing 3.1: Definition of `bigint`

```
1  typedef std::vector<unsigned char> bigint;
```

In this data structure, a digit is one byte. A vector is a good choice because it allows for random access, appending from both the front and back, and unbounded length. But the utility of the class lays in its methods not its data structure. We look at those next.

3.3 `bigint` addition

Addition of big integers involves writing out precisely the algorithm learned in elementary school. A listing follows which implements this algorithm for an unsigned `bigint`.

Listing 3.2: `bigint` Addition

```cpp
 1  bigint operator+(const bigint& lhs,
 2                   const bigint& rhs) {
 3    bigint sum;
 4    auto carry = 0;
 5    auto push_term = [&carry, &sum]
 6       (unsigned char lhs, unsigned char rhs) {
 7      unsigned int value = lhs + rhs + carry;
 8      unsigned char term = value & 0xff;
 9      carry = (value - term) ? 1 : 0;
10      sum.emplace(sum.begin(), term);
11    };
12
13    auto lhs_itr = lhs.rbegin();
14    auto rhs_itr = rhs.rbegin();
15    while (lhs_itr != lhs.rend() &&
16           rhs_itr != rhs.rend()) {
17      push_term(*lhs_itr++, *rhs_itr++);
18    }
19    while (lhs_itr != lhs.rend()) {
20      push_term(*lhs_itr++, 0);
21    }
22    while (rhs_itr != rhs.rend()) {
23      push_term(*rhs_itr++, 0);
24    }
25    if (carry) push_term(0, 0);
26    return sum;
27  }
```

The algorithm begins by with the least significant digits of each operand. We initialize a carry value to 0. Each iteration begins by adding together two bytes and the carry value. This is accomplished by push_term. The value overflows a byte exactly when there is a carry of value 0x01 from this digit to the next. We memo the result, shift the carry to the right, and iterate on the next set of bytes.

Since we visit every digit location exactly once, we have a linear time algorithm.

3.4 **bigint** negation

To represent signed bigints we will use the following simple extension of bigint.

Listing 3.3: Definition of signed bigint

```
1  struct signed_bigint {
2    bool negative = false;
3    bigint value;
4  };
```

The reason we do not represent signed bigint with twos complement is to avoid the difficulty in handling overflow in the addition and multiplication operators.

Lets revisit addition for signed arbitrary precision integers.

Listing 3.4: **bigint** Signed Addition

```
1  signed_bigint operator+(const signed_bigint& lhs,
2                          const signed_bigint& rhs) {
3    if (lhs.negative == rhs.negative) {
4      signed_bigint retval;
5      retval.negative = lhs.negative;
6      retval.value = lhs.value + rhs.value;
7      return retval;
8    }
9    if (rhs.negative) {
10     return subtract(lhs.value, rhs.value);
11   }
12   return subtract(rhs.value, lhs.value);
13 }
```

Above we use the function `subtract`, which we implement next. This is done by leveraging the twos complement of a sequence of bits.

For a 32-bit integer, the twos complement of a value b is the binary representation of the following operation.

$$\left(2^{32} - b\right) \,\&\, 0\text{xffff}$$

Note we are simply taking the difference from a larger number and masking the lower 32 bits. A simple way of determining the twos complement of an integer x is to negate its bits and add 1 to the result allowing overflow, which is equivalent to the operation above.

The important aspect of the twos complement is that addition of signed values need little special casing when precision is fixed. It is simply normal addition. It is that fact that we want to leverage in arbitrary precision arithmetic.

The following listing calculates the twos complement of a `bigint`. Observe that after flipping the bits and adding one, we must check if a carry occurred on the most significant bit. That is we must make sure to allow overflow when taking the twos complement in arbitrary precision integers.

Listing 3.5: bigint Twos Complement

```
1  bigint twos_complement(const bigint& b) {
2    bigint retval(b);
3    for (auto& node: retval) {
4      node = ~node;
5    }
6    retval = retval + bigint({0x1});
7    if (retval.size() > b.size()) {
8      retval.erase(retval.begin());
9    }
10   return retval;
11 }
```

When taking the twos complement, we need to be concerned with the fact that different values may have different lengths. Any unsigned bigint that differs from another with leading zero bytes are the same. However, with twos complement bigint, {0x0ff} ≠ {0xff}. The first is positive and the second is negative. This problem only arises with leading zero bytes. Because of this we need to pad positive values that have the most significant bit set with a zero byte. This will be done prior to calling twos_complement in subtraction.

To determine whether or not a value signed by twos complement is negative we check if the most significant bit of the value is set. As this will be useful, let us make this check a function of a bigint.

Listing 3.6: Most Significant Bit is Set

```
1  bool msb_set(const bigint& b) {
2    return b[0] & 0x80;
3  }
```

We are ready to implement subtraction of unsigned bigints using twos complement.

Listing 3.7: `bigint` Subtraction by Twos Complement

```
1  signed_bigint subtract(bigint lhs, bigint rhs) {
2    if (msb_set(lhs)) lhs.emplace(lhs.begin(), 0x00);
3    if (msb_set(rhs)) rhs.emplace(rhs.begin(), 0x00);
4    while (lhs.size() > rhs.size()) {
5      rhs.emplace(rhs.begin(), 0x00);
6    }
7    while (rhs.size() > lhs.size()) {
8      lhs.emplace(lhs.begin(), 0x00);
9    }
10   rhs = twos_complement(rhs);
11   signed_bigint retval;
12   retval.value = lhs + rhs;
13   if (retval.value.size() > lhs.size()) {
14     retval.value.erase(retval.value.begin());
15   }
16   retval.negative = msb_set(retval.value);
17   if (retval.negative) {
18     retval.value = twos_complement(retval.value);
19   }
20   while (retval.value.size() > 1 &&
21          !retval.value[0]) {
22     retval.value.erase(retval.value.begin());
23   }
24   return retval;
25 }
```

The preamble insures that the two `bigint` arguments are of the
same length and that neither represents a negative value as a twos
complement. We then take the twos complement of the second,
and add them. Afterward, we drop the overflow and convert from
a negative twos complement value to a `signed_bigint`. This
algorithm is linear in the size of its input.

3.5   `bigint` multiplication

We conclude with a discussion of multiplication of `bigint`s. Since
the sign of the result of multiplication has no affect on the descriptive
code, we restrict ourselves to unsigned `bigint` in the following. As

with addition, a naive implementation of multiplication translates
the elementary school algorithm to code.

```
   Listing 3.8: bigint Multiplication

 1  bigint operator*(const bigint& lhs,
 2                   const bigint& rhs) {
 3    auto mult_term = [] (const bigint& lhs,
 4                         unsigned char term) {
 5      bigint prod;
 6      unsigned char carry = 0;
 7      for (auto itr = lhs.rbegin();
 8           itr != lhs.rend();
 9           ++itr) {
10        unsigned int value = (*itr * term) + carry;
11        prod.emplace(prod.begin(), value & 0xff);
12        carry = value >> 8;
13      }
14      if (carry) {
15        prod.emplace(prod.begin(), carry);
16      }
17      return prod;
18    };
19    bigint prod;
20    for (auto& val : rhs) {
21      bigint term = mult_term(lhs, val);
22      prod.push_back(0x00);
23      prod = prod + term;
24    }
25    while (prod.size() > 1 && !prod[0]) {
26      prod.erase(prod.begin());
27    }
28    return prod;
29  }
```

The algorithm is similar to bigint addition in that there is a main
helper function that operates on digits. The only notable change
is that we insure there is no negative zero representation prior to
completion.

This is a quadratic algorithm, since for each digit in one operand
we examine every digit in the other. We can speed this up using

Karatsuba's algorithm.

3.6 Faster multiplication for `bigint`

Anatolii Alexeevitch Karatsuba was the first theoretician to break the quadratic barrier for multiplication. His algorithm is based on the following observation. Consider bytes written as the sum of two nibbles $a = a_1 * 2^4 + a_0$ and $b = b_1 * 2^4 + b_0$. Then we can write the product using the FOIL method.

$$a * b = a_1 * b_1 * 2^8 + (a_0 * b_1 + a_1 * b_0) * 2^4 + a_0 * b_0$$

This requires four multiplications in addition to the shifts. But if we arrange it so that $p = a_1 * b_1$, $q = a_0 * b_0$, and $r = (a_1 + a_0) * (b_1 + b_0) - q - p$. Then we have

$$a * b = p * 2^8 + r * 2^4 + q$$

That is we need only 3 multiplications instead of 4. So we have a speed up of 4/3. This small change is easy to implement. More importantly, we can apply this recursively, resulting in the following $O(n^{\lg 3})$ algorithm that calls a recursive sub-method on unsigned big integers.

Listing 3.9: `bigint` Multiplication by Karatsuba's Algorithm

```
1  bigint karatsuba(bigint lhs, bigint rhs) {
2    if (lhs.size() > rhs.size()) {
3      rhs.insert(rhs.begin(),
4                 lhs.size() - rhs.size(),
5                 0);
6    }
7    if (rhs.size() > lhs.size()) {
8      lhs.insert(lhs.begin(),
9                 rhs.size() - lhs.size(),
10                0) ;
11   }
12   return karatsuba_recursive(lhs, rhs);
13 }
```

Above, we pad the operands so that they are of the same size. This is done only for convenience of splitting during the recursive loop.

The recursive loop for Karatsuba's algorithm can be implemented without considering the sign of the operands as p, q and r are always positive. All that is needed is a direct translation of the insight above and a stopping rule.

Listing 3.10: Karatsuba's Algorithm

```
1  bigint karatsuba_recursive(
2      const bigint& lhs,
3      const bigint& rhs) {
4      if (!lhs.size()) return {0x00};
5      if (lhs.size() == 1) return lhs * rhs;
6      auto length = lhs.size() / 2;
7      bigint a1(lhs.begin(), lhs.begin() + length);
8      bigint a0(lhs.begin() + length, lhs.end());
9      bigint b1(rhs.begin(), rhs.begin() + length);
10     bigint b0(rhs.begin(), rhs.begin() + length);
11     bigint p = karatsuba_recursive(a1, b1);
12     bigint q = karatsuba_recursive(a0, b0);
13     bigint r =
14       karatsuba_recursive(a1 + a0, b1 + b0) - q - p;
15     p.insert(p.end(), length * 2, 0x00);
16     r.insert(r.end(), length, 0x00);
17     return p + r + q;
18  }
```

Karatsuba's algorithm is not the asymptotically fastest known for multiplication. Indeed there are algorithms based on the Fast Fourier Transform that achieve better run time guarantees. However, when a fast multiplication algorithm is needed in practice, Karatsuba's does very well.

Chapter 4

Fibonacci

The Fibonacci sequence is familiar to every computer scientist. It is one of the first recursively defined sequences we encounter.

Recall the Fibonacci sequence is the series of number starting with 0 and 1 such that the nth term is the sum of its previous two terms. Formally, the series F is defined as:

$$F(0) = 0; F(1) = 1$$
$$F(n) = F(n-1) + F(n-2)$$

It pops up again and again, from discussions of the golden ratio to optimization in heap access. And it provides interviewers with a great sequence of questions, since its simplicity can often lead careless candidate astray. This chapter looks in depth at many techniques for producing the Fibonacci sequence.

4.1   Naive recursive solution

Let us proceed as if we are asked to code up a method that returns the nth Fibonacci number. There are many ways to write Fibonacci sequence, and the following is not one you should ever put up on the whiteboard.

Listing 4.1: Fibonacci

```
1  unsigned fib(unsigned n) {
2    if (n == 0) return 0;
3    if (n == 1) return 1;
4    return fib(n-1) + fib(n-2);
5  }
```

When it terminates, this code will correctly produce the nth Fibonacci number, but its running time is an exponential function of n. The reason is because the program is doing the same work over and over again. To see this, let's count the number of recursive calls the program makes as a function of n. If n is 0 or 1 there is but a single call which returns in line 2 or 3. Now for $n = 2$, we have 2 recursive calls, first $F(n-1) = F(1)$ then $F(n-2) = F(0)$ in line 4. For $n = 3$, we call $F(3-1) = F(2)$ for 2 more recursive calls, and $F(3-2) = F(1)$ for one more. Continuing in this way, we see that the number of calls produces the sequence $1, 1, 2, 3, 5, 8, 13...$ which is again the Fibonacci sequence. It was Johannes Kepler who first showed that this sequence grows exponentially by proving that $F(n+1)/F(n) \to \frac{1}{2}(\sqrt{5}+1)$. A fact we revisit later.

4.2   Memoization

The problem is that in the recursive calculation for $F(n-1)$ we need to calculate $F(n-2)$. But after this calculation we are asking the function to again calculate $F(n-2)$. So we are doing the same work twice. This can be alleviated with *memoization* , or keeping track of intermediary calculations to use again later. With this idea we can write a linear version of our program.

Listing 4.2: Fibonacci with Memoization

```cpp
unsigned fib(unsigned n) {
  std::vector<unsigned> memo(n+1);
  for (size_t i = 0; i <= n; ++i) {
    if (0 == i) memo[i] = 0;
    else if (1 == i) memo[i] = 1;
    else memo[i] = memo[i-1] + memo[i-2];
  }
  return memo[n];
}
```

Since the 44th Fibonacci number (701408733) is larger than max-int on a 32 bit machine there isn't worry about a dynamic data structure growing too large. Memoization could have been used in a recursive implementation as well, but it would have been wise to pass the memo vector by reference. To see that it has linear run time, note that the number of intermediate calculations is the same as the sequence number we are asked to compute.

4.3 Iterative solution

Now we focus on minor improvements. For those with an eye to reducing memory usage, we can see that only the last two entries of the memo need to be kept. That is for Fibonacci, full memorization is unnecessary. We need memo only the last two trailing values of the sequence. Implementing this idea we have the following listing.

```
Listing 4.3: Fibonacci Iterative
1  unsigned fib(unsigned n) {
2    if (0 == n) return 0;
3    if (1 == n) return 1;
4    unsigned cur = 0;
5    unsigned trailing = 1;
6    for(size_t i = 0; i < n; ++i) {
7      unsigned temp = cur;
8      cur = cur + trailing;
9      trailing = temp;
10   }
11   return cur;
12 }
```

Note it is still linear, as we calculate one Fibonacci value in each iteration. It is also a forward calculation, working bottom up instead of top down. This is the difference between recursive and iterative solutions.

4.4   Tail recursion

We've created an iterative program and abandoned the naive recursive call. But there is another optimization that will take us back to recursion. Tail recursion is an optimization in which the recursion can be unrolled. In order to make use of it here, we will need to make use of helper function. The helper function will hold the current and trailing values of the sequence in the parameter list. It is defined inline.

To implement this version, we call the tail recursive helper function with the properly initialized arguments.

Listing 4.4: Fibonacci Tail Recursion

```
1  unsigned fib_tail_recursion(unsigned n,
2                               unsigned fib0,
3                               unsigned fib1) {
4    if (1 == n) return fib1;
5    return fib_tail_recursion(n-1, fib1, fib0 +fib1);
6
7  }
8  unsigned fib(unsigned n){
9    if (0 == n) return 0;
10   return fib_tail_recursion(n, 0, 1);
11 }
```

The tail recursion is actually working iteratively, but with a recursive signature.

4.5 Direct computation

We leave the Fibonacci sequence with a trick bound to impress anyone asking this question. Unless you're familiar with recurrence relations, it is a shock to many that we can do better than liner. In fact Fibonacci n can be computed directly in logarithmic time. The reason for this is that there is a closed form formula for the nth Fibonacci number, used to derive the recurrence relation below.

$$F_n = \frac{\phi^n - \psi^n}{\sqrt{5}}; \phi = \frac{1 + \sqrt{(5)}}{2}; \psi = \frac{1 - \sqrt{5}}{2}$$

Since exponentiation to the power n takes $O(\log n)$ calculations, we can use rounding to calculate the nth Fibonacci number directly with the promised run time bounds..

Listing 4.5: Fibonacci Closed Form

```
1  unsigned fib(unsigned n) {
2      double positive_golden_ratio = 1 + sqrt(5.);
3      double negative_golden_ratio = 1 - sqrt(5.);
4      double pos_pow = pow(positive_golden_ratio, n);
5      double neg_pow = pow(negative_golden_ratio, n);
6      double numerator = pos_pow - neg_pow;
7      double denominator = pow(2., n) * sqrt(5.);
8      return (unsigned) (numerator/denominator);
9  }
```

The careful reader will note that we are using implicit rounding from a double to an integer in the return value. However, for the first many sequence values of fib this rounding gives an accurate number. On my system, the first discrepancy comes at the 72nd Fibonacci number, where the difference is one. So this floating-point method can compute more sequence points than integer based solutions.

Chapter 5

Primality Testing

Prime numbers are the elements of number theory. As integers with no other divisor than themselves, they are simple to define. But the primes have a structure and depth that have piqued mankind's interest for centuries.

One simple to state problem is deciding whether or not a value is a prime. This problem has been studied since the time of the ancient Greeks. In a great breakthrough, a polynomial time solution to this problem has been found. But it still makes a good programming problem, as there are many insights and shortcuts that can be discovered when looking at the problem.

In this chapter we look at three approaches to the problem of primality testing. We begin by discussing the naive solution. We then look at efficient implementations of the Sieve of Eratosthenes. Finally, in the conclusion we will examine the Miller-Rabin randomized primality test.

5.1 Naive primality testing

A straightforward implementation of primality testing tests whether or not any value less than the parameter n divides evenly. For large values, it is inefficient to attempt to test every smaller value. A better implementation of primality testing will first take steps to reduce the number of tests made.

For instance, it is clear that if there is a value that factors into the parameter, than there must be value must be less than or equal to the square root of the parameter. So we need no check every value, just those between 2 and $\sqrt{n}$. And in that range, aside from two no other even value need be tested. With these observations we have our first primality test.

```
1  bool isprime(unsigned n) {
2    if (0 == n || 1 == n) return false;
3    auto sqroot = sqrt(n);
4    if (2 <= sqroot && 0 == n % 2) return false;
5    for (int index = 3; index <= sqroot; index += 2) {
6      if (0 == n % index) return false;
7    }
8    return true;
9  }
```

Can we do better? For small values, the answer is yes but at the cost of space.

5.2   The sieve of Eratosthenes

The inefficiency of the naive algorithm is due to the redundant checking of factors. We already noted that once 2 has been ruled out as a factor it is clear that no even value can be a factor. Similarly once 3 has been ruled out, then all multiples of three have been ruled out. What we are discovering is called the sieve of Eratosthenes. That is once we know all the primes less than a certain value, the next prime is simply the next value that is not a multiple of any of these.

As we already noted we need not check values above $\sqrt{n}$. Implementing the sieve, we need to be concerned with tracking known non-factors above $\sqrt{n}$. In the following listing, we use a bit vector to track discovered primes.

Listing 5.2: Primality Testing With Sieve of Eratosthenes

```
1  bool isprime(unsigned n) {
2    if (n < 2) return false;
3    std::vector<bool> known_prime(sqrt(n), true);
4    for (size_t val = 2;
5         val <= known_prime.size();
6         ++val) {
7      if (known_prime[val]) {
8        if (0 == (n % val)) return false;
9        for (auto multiple = val * val;
10            multiple < known_prime.size();
11            multiple += val) {
12          known_prime[multiple] = false;
13        }
14      }
15    }
16    return true;
17  }
```

Note that we can start at the square of the current value since every small factor of that value has already been memoized by smaller factors.

The sieve trades space for time, by allowing a fast addition operation to replace an expensive division operation. But since we have memoized the sieve, the data calculated above can be reused.

5.3   A heap based approach to the sieve of Eratosthenes

An attempt to reduce the amount of space used can be made. For instance, a heap provides an efficient data structure to hold the largest evaluated possible factor of n . Once we find that the top of the heap misses a value, we know that value is a prime.

Listing 5.3: Primality Testing With Sieve of Eratosthenes

```
1  bool isprime(unsigned n) {
2    if (n == 2) return true;
3    if (n < 2 || 0 == (n % 2)) return false;
4    auto sqroot = sqrt(n);
5    typedef std::pair<unsigned,
6                      unsigned> seive_entry;
7    std::vector<seive_entry> primes;
8    primes.push_back({4,2});
9    unsigned current = primes.front().second;
10   while (current <= sqroot) {
11     auto front = primes.front().first;
12     if ((front - 2) == current) {
13       unsigned prime = front - 1;
14       if (0 == (n % prime)) return false;
15       primes.push_back({prime * prime, prime});
16       std::make_heap(primes.begin(),
17                      primes.end(),
18                      std::greater<seive_entry>());
19     }
20     current = front;
21     std::pop_heap(primes.begin(),
22                   primes.end(),
23                   std::greater<seive_entry>());
24     primes.back().first += primes.back().second;
25     std::push_heap(primes.begin(),
26                    primes.end(),
27                    std::greater<seive_entry>());
28   }
29   return true;
30 }
```

A problem with the above implementation is that the number of primes increases, the number of values that are compared against current increases. At large value of n, we lose any performance gain we had from avoiding the division to the large number of comparisons.

5.4 The Miller-Rabin randomized primality test

An solution to primality testing efficient in expectation was first found from the study of random algorithms. Named after its authors, it is Miller-Rabin primality test.

This test is simple to code, but technical to understand. It relies on the following theorem proven by the authors. Suppose that $n > 3$ is an odd number, and we write $n - 1 = 2^s \cdot d$ for natural numbers s and d. The theorem stats that n is not prime if there exists an a such that the following equations hold.

$$a^d \not\equiv 1 \; (\mod n)$$
$$a^{2^r d} \not\equiv -1 \; (\mod n) \text{ for all } 0 \leq r \leq s - 1$$

Miller and Rabin showed that when n is composite, over $3/4$ of the values from 2 to $n - 2$ satisfy those equations. When n is prime, none due. So a test made with a value chosen random from that range has a high probability of success

The following listing implements this algorithm.

Listing 5.4: Primality testing with the Miller-Rabin random algorithm

```cpp
bool isprime(unsigned n) {
  if (2 == n || 3 == n) return true;
  if (n < 2 || 0 == (n % 2)) return false;
  auto s = 0;
  auto d = n - 1;
  while (0 == (d % 2)) {
    s++;
    d /= 2;
  }
  std::uniform_int_distribution<unsigned> dist(
      2,
      n-2);
  for (auto i = 0; i < 3; ++i) {
    auto a = dist(rng);
    auto x = ((unsigned) pow(a, d)) % n;
    if (1 == x || (n - 1) == x) continue;
    for (auto j = 1; j < s; ++j) {
      x = (x * x) % n;
      if (1 == x) return false;
      if ((n - 1) == x) break;
    }
    if ((n - 1) == x) continue;
    return false;
  }
  return true;
}
```

Note that the above algorithm can make only one kind of error. When n is composite, it is unlikely that a false positive will be reported. However when n is prime, the Miller-Rabin test is always correct. We can reduce the error at the cost of increased run time by running the test multiple times and reporting a value is composite if ever any run reports it composite.

In conclusion we mention that the AKS (Agrawal, Kayal, Saxena) primality test is a strongly polynomial deterministic algorithm discovered in 2002. While a great achievement, discussion of that algorithm is much more technical than that required for the Miller-Rabin test above, will need to wait until another edition.

Chapter 6

Powers and Roots

After our brief diversion into number theory, we return to more standard fare from numerical algorithms. We examine two problems. We first look at exponentiation of an integral exponent, and second the problem of calculating the root of a value.

Formally both are exponentiation, but we will see these two problems have much different solutions. And while the first provides us a utility function that can be used in my other solutions, the second is deeper and leads to exploration of one of the fastest converging iterative solutions in numerical programming.

6.1   Exponentiation

To begin with exponentiation, we ask for an algorithm to calculate x^y for integral y. This is a commonly asked question, because it can be answered with naive inefficiency or with a clever use of recursion.

The naive solution applies successive multiplication. Starting with a return value of 1, while the exponent is positive we multiply the result by x and decrease y by a unit. Note there is one special case to consider, since $0^1 = 0$. This is handled in the listing below.

Listing 6.1: Naive Exponentiation

```
1  int pow(int x, unsigned y) {
2    if (0 == x && 0 != y) return 0;
3    int retval = 1;
4    while (y--) {
5      retval = retval * x;
6    }
7    return retval;
8  }
```

We call this the naive solution because it takes time linear in the number of iterations.

6.2 Successive squaring

Successive squaring is an approach that reduces the amount of calculation required to a logarithmic number of iterations.

The technique is derived from the following observation. If y is even, then there exists z such that $y = 2z$. Then $x^y = x^{2z} = x^z * x^z$. Alternatively, if y is odd then we can write $y = 2z + 1$ and $x^y = x^z * x^z * x$. In either case, calculating of x^z is simpler than x^y. We can continue to recursively simplify until we are left with either $z = 0$ or 1.

A recursive implementation of this idea is presented in the following listing.

Listing 6.2: Exponentiation by Successive Squaring

```
1  int pow(int x, unsigned y) {
2    if (0 == y) return 1;
3    auto val = pow(x, y/2);
4    if (0 == y % 2) {
5      return val * val;
6    }
7    return x * val * val;
8  }
```

Note that we must be careful to memoize the recursive calculation of $x^{y/2}$ to avoid return pow(x, $y/2$) twice as doing so we affect multiple identical calculations. This was the same pitfall encountered with the naive approach to calculating Fibonacci numbers.

In our final encounter with exponentiation we develop an iterative solution. As we see shortly, the functions developed studying bit flipping are of use.

An iterative solution must start with what is known, which is only x. By repeatedly squaring x we calculate x^2, from x^2 we can calculate x^4 and so on. Now consider the binary representation of the value y. Suppose $y = 6$, then the binary representation of $y = 2^2 + 2^1 = \text{0x110}$. So $x^y = x^4 * x^2$. If we know the powers of x that are themselves powers of 2, we can produce x^y from the binary representation of y. This leads in the natural way to an iterative solution.

This is presented in the listing below.

Listing 6.3: Exponentiation by Successive Squaring Iteratively

```
1  int pow(int x, unsigned y) {
2      std::vector<int> memo(log_x(y)+2);
3      memo[0] = 1;
4      memo[1] = x;
5      for (auto index = 2;
6              index < memo.size();
7              ++index) {
8          memo[index] = memo[index - 1] *
9                          memo[index - 1];
10     }
11     int retval = memo[0];
12     while(y) {
13         auto pos = 1+log_x(lowest_set_bit(y));
14         retval *= memo[pos];
15         y = clear_last_bit(y);
16     };
17     return retval;
18 }
```

The vector memo holds the values of x to the power 2^{index}. We need as many as $log(y) + 1$, as well as the value at index 0.

At first glance, the iterative solution seems opposite of the recursive solution. In the recursive solution we calculate from the top down; dividing, simplifying, and recursing. In the iterative solution we calculate from the bottom up, successively squaring until enough information is known to construct the answer. However study will show that these two solutions are doing equivalent work.

6.3   Integer approximation of the square root

We now turn our attention to fractional exponents. To avoid complications from early generalization, lets look at solving the problem of calculating the square root of a value.

When asked to calculate the square root of a number, most being immediately writing a binary search for finding the integer approximation for the root. A decent approach is binary search.

Listing 6.4: Integer Square Root

```
1  unsigned int sqrt(unsigned int x) {
2    if (0 == x) return 0;
3    int lower = 1;
4    int higher = x;
5    while (higher > lower) {
6      int test = lower + (higher-lower) / 2;
7      if (test*test > x) {
8        if (test == higher) break;
9        higher = test;
10     } else {
11       if (test == lower) break;
12       lower = test;
13     }
14   }
15   return lower;
16 }
```

There are some good things to note about this code. For integers, the domain of *sqrt* is only over positive numbers. The requirement to process only over positive integers is built into the function prototype. Secondly, binary search is implemented correctly so as to find the first integer equal to or lower than the actual square root.

6.4 Binary search to the square root

Consider asking to find the square root for decimal numbers, not simply integers. This requires two changes in the algorithm above.

First, the input domain has changed character. For integers, the approximation is either 0 or some number greater than or equal to one. But for decimal numbers, the domain increases to contain the interval $(0, 1)$. This requires care, since in this region $x^2 < x$. So if we remain with binary search, we must have a different update rule and different starting bounds.

Secondly, we must now consider arithmetic with decimal integers. Note C/C++ does not have unsigned floating-point numbers. Hence we need to have some kind of error handling.

Also we must consider a stopping rule. In the binary search above, we could stop when the upper bound and lower bound cross. This was inevitable and quick when we dealt with integer values. But with decimals, comparisons should be done with deltas. To this end, we must implement a check to see if the candidate value is within epsilon ϵ of the target. This defines a delta for equality comparison.

Putting it all together, we have the listing for our next version of the square root method.

```
     Listing 6.5: Decimal Square Root
 1  double sqrt(double x) {
 2    if (x < 0) return -1.0;
 3    if (x == 1) return 1.0;
 4    double higher = (x < 1) ? 1 : x;
 5    double lower = (x < 1) ? x : 1;
 6    while ((higher - lower) > epsilon) {
 7      double test = lower + (higher - lower) / 2;
 8      double eval = test * test;
 9      if (eval > x) {
10        higher = test;
11      } else {
12        lower = test;
13      }
14    }
15    return lower;
16  }
```

This is an efficient solution. The rate of convergence depends on the epsilon chosen. To find $\sqrt{n}$, this algorithm is an implementation of binary search over $\epsilon^{-1} * n$ buckets, resulting in a logarithmic algorithm.

6.5   Newton's method for the square root

To do better we enlist an advanced technique for solving inverse problems called Newton's method. This algorithm was discovered first by Isaac Newton and later simplified by Joseph Raphson. While discussion of this method involves a small amount of calculus, it provides an efficient solution to finding roots of any well behaved function.

To be precise, given a function $f(x)$, Newton's method provides a way for finding a value x such that $f(x) = 0$. Such a value x is called a root of $f(x)$. Newton's method is an iterative algorithm, which starting at a guess, uses the tangent line of f at x to revises the guess towards a root. The update rule is

$$x_{n+1} = x_n - f(x_n)/f'(x_n)$$

To see how this is derived, consider staring at θ_0. The function evaluates θ_0 to $f(\theta_0)$, and the tangent line intercepts the point $(\theta_0, f(\theta_0))$ with slope $f'(\theta_0)$. The tangent line intercepts the x-axis at θ_1. Iterating again on θ_1 we walk along successive approximations towards a root of $f(x)$.

To apply Newton's method for finding a square root of some number y, we consider the function $f(x) = x^2 - y$. Since for any application y is constant, the derivative of this function is $f'(x) = 2x$. Putting this together, we need to iterate the simple update rule

$$x_{n+1} = x_n - (x_n^2 - y)/2x_n$$

For $\sqrt{1/2} \approx 0.707$, the following graph shows the first two updates starting at $x_0 = 0.75$. Note how close the approximation is to the x-axis after only two iterations.

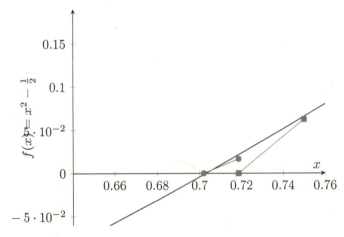

As we saw with all iterations involving decimals, we must again implement a stopping rule. For this problem we can choose an threshold in which $|x_{n+1} - x_n| < \epsilon$ or a threshold in which $|y - x_n^2| < \epsilon$. Either will suffice, we use the later.

Implementing the update rule from above we have the following listing.

Listing 6.6: Decimal Square Root from Newton's Method

```cpp
double sqrt(double y) {
    if (y < 0) return -1.0;
    double x = y;
    while (std::abs(y - x * x) > epsilon) {
        x = x - (x*x - y) / (2 * x);
    }
    return x;
}
```

For fractional exponent's, Newton's method guarantees a quadratic rate of convergence. That is, in every iteration the error decreases by a quadratic function of the previous error.

Since Newton's method can be used to approximate any decimal exponentiation, this method generalized to an elegant general solution to the problem of calculating exponentiation.

Chapter 7

Geometric Distance

Geometric questions are interesting because they facilitate the development of an idea from basic principles. For instance, asking to find the distance from a point to a line requires the definition of data structures to represent with a point and a line, finding a segment originating at a point and perpendicular to the line, and finally determining the length. There is geometric intuition, mathematical rigor, and the opportunity to translate formula into code.

The principles for geometric questions asked for are usually basic; definitions of points and vectors, Euclidean distance, the dot product. From two-body distance to nearest neighbors, questions of geometric distance are rich. And while rare, at times they digress towards the ideas of the cross product, the convex hull of points, and triangulation. And when they do, this and the following chapters should provide a good study guide.

7.1   Definitions

When working with geometric objects, the first problem to solve is how to represent the data. We will represent points in space by a vector originating at the origin. The simplest vector will contain two `double` members x and y. But a good structure to represent a two dimensional vector should have a number of other member functions. At a minimum these should be scalar multiplication, vector addition, and the dot product. Another common property of a vector is its length. The structure below is a minimal solution to this problem that supports these four operations. With these members defined, other operators such as scalar multiplication from the left and vector subtraction are simple to define.

Listing 7.1: Definition of a vector

```
 1  struct vector {
 2    double x;
 3    double y;
 4    vector operator*(const double& scalar) const {
 5      return {x * scalar, y * scalar};
 6    }
 7    vector operator+(const vector& rhs) const {
 8      return {x + rhs.x , y + rhs.y};
 9    }
10    double dot(const vector& rhs) const {
11      return (x * rhs.x) + (y * rhs.y);
12    }
13    double length() const {
14      return sqrt(x * x + y * y);
15    }
16  };
```

A few words are in order about the dot product. Recall that for vectors $\vec{a}$ and $\vec{b}$, we have $\vec{a} \cdot \vec{b} = |\vec{a}||\vec{b}| \cos \theta$, where θ is the angle between the vectors. Specifically, when two vectors are perpendicular the dot product is 0. And when two unit vectors are parallel the dot product is 1.

Although points and vectors are not the same, it will simplify things later to represent them with the same structure. We will distinguish when operations act on vectors and points when it is necessary.

A unit vector is a vector of length 1. It is commonly used for specifying a direction of a line or the tangent of a plane. The following function normalizes a vector to unit length. The only special case to consider is if the vector is of zero length, for which there is not specified conversion.

Listing 7.2: Unit Vector

```
1  vector unit_vector(const vector& v) {
2      if (v.x == 0 && v.y == 0) return v;
3      auto length = v.length();
4      return {v.x / length, v.y / length};
5  }
```

Recall that a line has the vector equation $\vec{a} + t\vec{u}$ where a is a point on the line and $\vec{u}$ is a unit vector. Here t is a scalar value that identifies a single point on the line. Inspired from this equation, a line will be represented by a point in space and a direction vector. The direction vector will be assumed to b a unit vector.

Listing 7.3: Definition of a line

```
1  struct line {
2      vector a;
3      vector u;
4  };
```

With this foundation, we will begin to approach some interesting programming problems.

7.2 Distance between a point and a line

To find the distance between a point and a line requires knowing how to calculate the distance between two points in space. The Euclidean distance d between the points $a = (x_a, y_a)$ and $b = (x_b, y_b)$ is

$$d(a, b) = \sqrt{(x_a - x_b)^2 + (y_a - y_b)^2}$$

We will make good use of the following function that evaluates this formula.

Listing 7.4: Distance Between Two Points

```
1  double distance(const vector& a, const vector& b) {
2    return sqrt(pow(a.x - b.x, 2)
3                + pow(a.y - b.y, 2));
4  }
```

The distance between a point and a line is the minimum distance between the point and any point on the line. Suppose a perpendicular is dropped from the point to the line, then the distance between the point and the intersection of the perpendicular is the minimum distance. To find the intersection, we work from first principles.

Suppose $\vec{p}$ is a point and the line is defined by $\vec{a} + t\vec{u}$, where $\vec{a}$ is a point on the line and $\vec{u}$ is a unit vector. Then $\vec{a} - \vec{p}$ is a vector from $\vec{p}$ to $\vec{a}$. The projection of this vector onto $\vec{u}$ gives the distance from a to the intersection of the line and the perpendicular. Using the dot product, we know length of the projection is $(\vec{a} - \vec{p}) \cdot \vec{u}$, and the vector is $\vec{n} = ((\vec{a} - \vec{p}) \cdot \vec{u})\vec{u}$. The perpendicular direction vector is then $(\vec{a} - \vec{p}) - \vec{n}$, from which we can get two points and the distance $||(\vec{a} - \vec{p}) - \vec{n}||$.

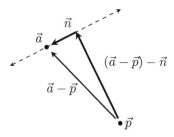

Translating this in to code is straightforward, made simpler by the vector operations defined above.

Listing 7.5: Distance Between a Point and a Line

```
1  double distance(const vector& p, const line& l) {
2      vector a_minus_p = l.a + (p * -1);
3      vector n = l.u * a_minus_p.dot(l.u);
4      vector perp = a_minus_p + (n * -1);
5      return perp.length();
6  }
```

7.3 Intersection of two lines

In two-dimensional Euclidean space, lines are either parallel or intersect. When they are parallel, to find the distance between them we can repeat of the subsection above with the point coming from one line and calculating the distance with the other.

Deciding whether or not two lines are parallel is a matter of taking the dot product. As mentioned above, two unit vectors are parallel exactly when their dot product is 1. Hence we have a simple solution for this problem.

Listing 7.6: Determine if Two Lines are Parallel

```
1  bool parallel(const line& s, const line& t) {
2      return std::abs(s.u.dot(t.u) - 1) < epsilon;
3  }
```

Notice that the dot product of two unit vectors is a decimal value, and hence we compare the value within an epsilon instead of by equality.

Now when two lines do intersect, it is interesting to find the point. This is a problem which tests how methodical and precise a solver is and whether or not she can translate arithmetic to code. Some of this question requires recall, and the candidate will spend most of her time calculating on the white board.

For parallel lines, the problem is determining if the lines are the same. This involves only solving for t for one line using the $\vec{a}$ in the other line, and then checking if the result is indeed $\vec{a}$.

Listing 7.7: Determine if Two Lines are Equal

```
1   bool operator==(const line& p, const line& q) {
2       if (!parallel(p, q)) return false;
3       auto t = 0.0;
4       if (0 != q.u.x) t = (p.a.x - q.a.x) / q.u.x;
5       else  t = (p.a.y - q.a.y) / q.u.y;
6       vector a = {q.a.x + t * q.u.x,
7                   q.a.y + t * q.u.y};
8       if (std::abs(a.x - p.a.x) < epsilon
9           && std::abs(a.y - p.a.y) < epsilon) {
10      return true;
11      }
12      return false;
13  }
```

For non-parallel lines the problem boils down to recalling that
the vector equation for a line is two simultaneous equations in
a single variable. Suppose that line p is given by the equation
$\vec{a_p} + t_p\vec{u_p}$, and line q is given by the equation $\vec{a_q} + t_q\vec{u_q}$. Then if
the two lines are not parallel the following equation has exactly one
solution.

$$\vec{a_p} + t_p\vec{u_p} = \vec{a_q} + t_q\vec{u_q}$$

This vector equation holds for all dimensions, so we can lift to
three dimensions. We can use the cross product to cancel t_q, since
$\vec{u} \times \vec{v} = |\vec{u}||\vec{v}| \sin\theta$, and since the vectors are the same we use $\theta = 0$
and recall $\sin 0 = 0$. This gives the following solution for t_p.

$$t_p\vec{u_q} \times \vec{u_p} = \vec{u_q} \times [\vec{a_q} - \vec{a_p}]$$

Working in two dimensions, the generalization of the cross product
is the determinant of the matrix formed by augmenting the vectors.
So we have the following identity.

$$\vec{u_q} \times \vec{u_p} = \begin{bmatrix} x_{u_p} \\ y_{u_p} \end{bmatrix} \times \begin{bmatrix} x_{u_q} \\ y_{u_q} \end{bmatrix} = \det \begin{bmatrix} x_{u_p} & x_{u_q} \\ y_{u_p} & y_{u_q} \end{bmatrix} = x_{u_p}y_{u_q} - x_{u_p}y_{u_q}$$

From this we can finally solve for t_p, which can be plugged into the
equation for p to give our solution.

$$t_p = \frac{1}{x_{u_p} y_{u_q} - x_{u_p} y_{u_q}} [x_{u_q}(y_{a_p} - y_{a_q}) - y_{u_q}(x_{a_p} - x_{a_q})]$$

While this was quite a lot of arithmetic, it is easily translated into code. The following method assumes that the lines are not parallel.

Listing 7.8: Determine the Intersection of Two Lines

```
1  vector intersection(const line& p, const line& q){
2      auto det = p.u.x * q.u.y - p.u.y * q.u.x;
3      auto t =
4          (q.u.x*(p.a.y-q.a.y)-q.u.y*(p.a.x-q.a.x))/det;
5      return {p.a.x + t * p.u.x, p.a.y + t * p.u.y};
6  }
```

We went to some lengths to generalize, but if the system of equations was solved instead by collecting terms and taking the inverse of the matrix the result is the same. However in that case the arithmetic becomes more egregious.

7.4 Nearest neighbors

We return to problems related to geometric distance by considering the following problem. Given a set $\mathbb{S}$ of n points in space, identify a point with its nearest neighbor in $\mathbb{S}$. This is known as the nearest neighbor problem.

The naive solution is to calculate the distance between every pair of points. Even though the number of calculations is half the number of pairs, this solution will require order n^2 distance calculations. However we can do better with just a little preprocessing, by building a kd-tree.

A kd-tree is a space partitioning data structure analogous to a binary search tree that allows for search over multiple dimensions. The abbreviation stands for k-dimensional tree. We will see that building the kd-tree takes $O(n \log n)$ time and lookup has logarithmic expected time. That is a significant improvement over testing a quadratic number of pairs.

The kd-tree data structure has two operations, `initialize` and `find`. Initialization builds the kd-tree from the given set of points. The idea is to build a search tree in which a comparison with a node in the tree divides the remaining search space in half. The nodes of the tree have the following structure.

Listing 7.9: Definition of kd-tree node

```
1  struct node {
2    vector point;
3    node* left = nullptr;
4    node* right = nullptr;
5    explicit node(vector point) : point(point) {}
6  };
```

The tree is built as follows. An order for the dimensions of the space is fixed and one dimension is assigned to each level of the tree. Now at a level, we find the median coordinate of the remaining points in the prescribed dimension. The points are then partitioned by their coordinate values into two sets, one of lesser value and one of greater. Those of lesser value are members of the recursively built left child kd-tree, and those of higher value are members of the recursively built right kd-tree.

To implement this behavior, we use the following class to compare vectors only in a single dimension. By constructing with the proper parameter we can alternate the dimension in which the points are compared. It is used as a functional by both kd-tree operations.

Listing 7.10: Fixed Dimension Comparator

```
1  class fixed_dim_compartor {
2  public:
3    fixed_dim_compartor(unsigned dim) : dim_(dim) {}
4    bool operator() (const vector& a,
5                     const vector&b) {
6      if (0 == dim_) return a.x < b.x;
7      return a.y < b.y;
8    }
9  private:
10   const unsigned dim_;
11 };
```

Implementation is then completed by calling a locally defined recursive functional called `build_kd_tree`. It is within this functional that the steps outlined above are taken.

Listing 7.11: Initialize a kd-tree

```
1  node* initialize(std::vector<vector> points) {
2    std::function<node*(
3        size_t,
4        std::vector<vector>::iterator,
5        std::vector<vector>::iterator)>
6      build_kd_tree = [&build_kd_tree] (
7        size_t dim,
8        std::vector<vector>::iterator begin,
9        std::vector<vector>::iterator end) {
10     if (begin == end) return (node*) nullptr;
11     auto mid = begin + (end - begin) / 2;
12     nth_element(begin, mid, end,
13                     fixed_dim_compartor(dim));
14     auto root = new node(*mid);
15     dim = (dim + 1) % 2;
16     root->left = build_kd_tree(dim, begin, mid);
17     root->right = build_kd_tree(dim, mid+1, end);
18     return root;
19   };
20   return build_kd_tree(0,
21                          points.begin(),
22                          points.end());
23 }
```

To use the kd-tree of find the nearest neighbor of a point p, the tree is walked downward from the root. Each branch decision is made on the same dimension used in creation, with a less than comparison branching left, and a greater than or equal to comparison branching right. Unlike retrieval in a binary search tree, at each level the branch node is saved in a stack. After the search completes, the distance from p to each point in the stack is calculated and compared with the desired value returned.

Listing 7.12: Find in a *k*d-tree

```
1  vector find(node* kd_tree, const vector& point) {
2    int dim = 0;
3    std::stack<vector> path;
4    while (nullptr != kd_tree) {
5      path.push(kd_tree->point);
6      kd_tree =
7        fixed_dim_compartor(dim)(kd_tree->point,
8                                 point)
9        ? kd_tree = kd_tree->right
10       : kd_tree = kd_tree->left;
11     dim = (dim + 1) % 2;
12   }
13   vector neighbor;
14   double min = std::numeric_limits<double>::max();
15   while (!path.empty()) {
16     if (path.top() == point) {
17       neighbor = path.top();
18       break;
19     };
20     auto dist = distance(path.top(), point);
21     if (dist <= min) {
22       min = dist;
23       neighbor = path.top();
24     }
25     path.pop();
26   }
27   return neighbor;
28 }
```

Notice during the final determination of the nearest neighbor we avoid equality. The problem was posed as a method to pair points with their nearest neighbor. However, in practice the set is composed of hubs and we have a series of points for which we want to find the nearest hub. Concretely, the set could be the location of post offices and the points could be homes.

Chapter 8

Triangles

Interesting geometry problems involve more than recalling the dot product and the straightforward implementation of a function for Euclidean distance. Instead they require a candidate to stretch his geometric intuition, discovering properties of points and shapes, and proving that his discovery is valid and efficient.

One line of questioning that allows a candidate to experience such discovery involves the process of triangulating a polygon. The line of questioning begins with considering the simple geometry of a triangle and leads to an efficient mechanism for calculating the convex hull of a polygon.

In this section, we will again restrict ourselves to two-dimensional space, and reuse many of the procedures we wrote in the previous section on geometry.

Let us begin with the question of how to calculate the area of a triangle.

8.1 Representation of a triangle

To calculate the area of a triangle, we first need to define a representation for a triangle. Triangles can have many representations; three points, three pairwise intersecting lines, a point and a non-adjacent segment. The simplest of these representations is three points in the plane. We find it more intuitive to talk about points instead of vectors. Below we have the listings for a point structure.

Listing 8.1: Definition of a Point

```
1 typedef vector point;
```

Using this, we define a triangle as a collection of three points.

Listing 8.2: Definition of a Triangle

```
1 struct triangle {
2    point a;
3    point b;
4    point c;
5    triangle(const point& a,
6            const point& b,
7            const point& c)
8      : a(a), b(b), c(c) {}
9 };
```

We have defined a constructor for convenience only.

8.2   Area of a triangle

To return to the motivating question, suppose we have a triangle defined by three points A, B, and C. Given the coordinates of three points, there are many ways to calculate the bounded area. For instance, recall that $Area(\triangle) = \frac{1}{2}b \times h$, where b is the length of the base and h is the height. With three points we can pick any two, say A and B, and call the segment AB the base. The length of the base is then simply $\|AB\|$. We can determine the height as the distance from the third point C to this segment using the code in the previous chapter.

But there is a simpler way. Recall given two points A and B the segment between them is the vector $AB = B - A$. Then given two segments AB and AC, the length of the cross product $AB \times AC$ is equal to the area of the parallelogram defined by the vectors. And as we can see, the area of the parallelogram is twice the area of the triangle defined by three points.

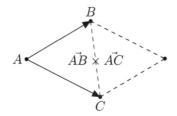

Continuing along these lines will be useful. Let us first define a structure for the vector defined by two points. Recall that a vector AB is the object such that if A and B are considered vectors instead of points, then $B = A + AB$.

So we need only calculate the cross product of the segments AB and AC. To convert this idea into code, recall that the length of the cross product is given by the formula below.

$$x_{AB} * y_{AC} - x_{AC} * y_{AB}$$

Notice that we must be consistent with which point we choose as vertex. That is we do not want to calculate $AB \times BC$. Also we must be careful about sign. The cross product follow the right hand rule, so the length may be positive or negative. In calculating area, the answer must be non-negative. Now with this in mind, using the definition of a vector above we can easily translate the equation into code.

Listing 8.3: Area of a Triangle

```
1  double area(const triangle& t) {
2      vector ab = t.b - t.a;
3      vector ac = t.c - t.a;
4      double a = 0.5 * (ab.x * ac.y - ab.y * ac.x);
5      return std::abs(a);
6  }
```

8.3 Triangulation

With the preliminaries out of the way, let us being an interesting line of questioning. Consider a triangle ABC and a point D in the

plane. How would you determine whether or not D was within
ABC?

As planned, the preliminaries lead to the answer. Suppose D is
within ABC. A triangulation of ABC with D is the decomposition
of the triangle into smaller triangles adjacent to D.

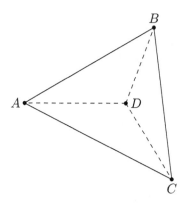

Drawing this simple picture is enough evidence to assert that if
D is within ABC then

$$Area(ABC) = Area(ABD) + Area(ADC) + Area(DBC)$$

And in fact, one is just as quick to see that the above equality
holds if and only if D is within ABC. Since otherwise, one of the
triangles adjacent to D must extend beyond ABC.

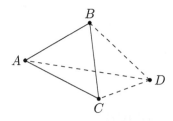

Since we can calculate $Area(ABC)$, the solution is simply a
matter of triangulating ABC and D.

Listing 8.4: Point in a Triangle

```cpp
bool point_in_triangle(const triangle& t,
                       const point& d) {
  double triange_area = area(t);
  triangle abd = triangle(d, t.a, t.b);
  triangle adc = triangle(d, t.a, t.c);
  triangle dbc = triangle(d, t.b, t.c);
  double sum = area(abd) + area(adc) + area(dbc);
  return std::abs(sum - triange_area) < epsilon;
}
```

8.4 Convex polygons

Consider a structure more complex than a triangle, say a convex polygon. A polygon is a figure bounded by a set of straight line segments. Because we can consider the exterior of the polygon to be composed of line segments drawn between any collection of points, a set $S = \{p_1, p_2, p_3...\}$ of three or more points defines a convex polygon C. What makes the polygon convex is that every interior point $p \in C$ can be written as the weighted sum of the defining points where the weights are non-negative and their sum is one. That is

$$p = \sum_i w_i p_i; \sum_i w_i = 1; w_i \geq 0 \text{ for all } i$$

For the geometrically minded, a polygon is convex if any straight line through an interior point intersection the boundary exactly twice.

Now suppose we have a convex polygon P defined by a vector of points S.

Listing 8.5: Definition of a Polygon

```cpp
typedef std::vector<point> polygon;
```

How would we test whether a point D was in the interior of P? If we proceed with care, we can successfully extend our method of triangulation above to answer this question. But to do this efficiently requires an advanced algorithm.

Generalizing the equation for hit testing above, we can determine whether or not D is in the interior of P by triangulating P with D and then comparing the sum of the areas of these triangles to the area of the convex polygon defined by P. We will find a challenge in both computing the area of the convex polygon as well as triangulation. But once we solve these questions, our solution is in hand.

8.5   Area of a convex polygon

Let us first tackle the problem of finding the area of a convex polygon. We know that if we have an interior point, the sum of the areas of the triangulation will equal the area of the polygon. Since we can calculate the area of a triangle, we set our sights on finding an interior point. This is our first sub problem.

8.5.1   An interior point

From the definition of the convex polygon, it is clear that we can find the center (x, y) of the polygon by taking the average of the sum of the coordinates of P in the horizontal and vertical directions.

$$x = \frac{1}{|S|} \sum_i p_i.x$$

$$y = \frac{1}{|S|} \sum_i p_i.y$$

So the solution to finding an interior point is not difficult, and we can write down a function to give us what we want with a single iteration of the points defining the polygon.

Listing 8.6: Interior Point of a Polygon

```
point center(const polygon& poly) {
    double x = 0.0;
    double y = 0.0;
    for (auto& p: poly) {
        x += p.x / poly.size();
        y += p.y / poly.size();
    }
    return {x,y};
}
```

But now when we go to compute the triangulation of P with the center point C, we run into a problem. With the triangle, we could just take any two vertexes and C. The reason that worked is because every set of two vertexes in a triangle are both adjacent to each other and on the exterior of the polygon. But our convex polygon is only specified as a collection of points. We need to find all points that are adjacent on the exterior of the polygon. We've run into the problem of finding the convex hull of a polygon.

8.5.2 The convex hull

Finding the convex hull seems like the problem of finding all the points which are the extreme points of the convex polygon in some direction. As such, it is specialized search problem.

As with nearest neighbors, one can see an immediate naive solution. Consider each point in turn, and compute vectors from that point to all the other points in the polygon. If for each point, all the computed vectors extend in an arc of less than or equal to 180 degrees, then we have discovered an extreme point.

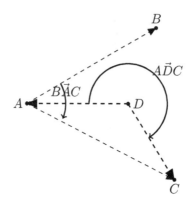

But consider the run time of this algorithm, a comparison of every node to every other node is an $O(n^2)$ algorithm. As usually, we can accomplish the search with $O(n \log n)$ steps in the worst case by implementing a clever search.

There has been much research in finding an optimal algorithm for computing the convex hull, and many solutions exist. Divide and conquer approaches are common, where the space is split in different dimensions and the extreme points are located. Another approach is to order the points in relation to some arbitrary starting element, and walk the enumeration looking for exterior points. This is the heart of to optimal solution called Graham's scan. Graham's scan was developed by Ronald Graham in 1972, and is the next algorithm we aim to implement.

Graham's scan works by starting at the extreme lower left hand corner of the polygon, and rotating counter-clockwise around the convex polygon. This is done by considering all the vectors extending from this extreme point to all other points in order of the angle they make with a line parallel to the x-axis passing through the extreme point.

Consider three points and their associated vectors. With these vectors it is simple to determine if the angle between them moves clockwise or counter-clockwise. As with the naive solution above, we can see the if we proceed in a counter-clockwise direction, then any time we make a clockwise turn we are moving towards the interior of the polygon.

The scan proceeds by adding the next vector to the list, then comparing the last three points in the list. If they make a clockwise turn, the second to last point added to the list is removed because that is an interior point. Else the algorithm iterates until all points have been considered.

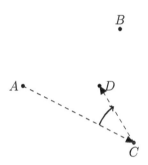

Figure 8.1: A clockwise angle means D is in the interior.

Note that the time complexity arrives only from the initial sort. After sorting, the scan is done linearly through the ordered list of points. Each point is either removed once or terminates a backward looking portion of the scan. As such it is $O(n \log n)$.

Translating Graham's discovery to code, we have the following.

Listing 8.7: Graham's Scan

```
1  polygon convex_hull(const polygon& poly) {
2      polygon out(poly);
3      point initial = poly[0];
4      for (auto& p: poly) {
5        if (p.y < initial.y ||
6            (p.y == initial.y && p.x < initial.x)) {
7          initial = p;
8        }
9      }
10     std::sort(out.begin(), out.end(),
11         [&initial] (const point& lhs,
12                     const point& rhs){
13       if (lhs == initial) return true;
14       if (rhs == initial) return false;
15       vector horizon = {1,0};
16       auto ulhs = unit_vector(lhs - initial);
17       auto urhs = unit_vector(rhs - initial);
18       auto diff = horizon.dot(ulhs) -
19                   horizon.dot(urhs);
20       if (diff > epsilon) return true;
21       else if (diff < -1 * epsilon) return false;
22       return lhs.length() < rhs.length();
23     });
24     for (int index=2; index < out.size(); ++index) {
25       while (out.size() > 3 &&
26              0 < sine_of_angle(out[index -2],
27                                out[index - 1],
28                                out[index])) {
29         out.erase(out.begin() + index - 1);
30         index = std::max(2, index - 1);
31       }
32     }
33     return out;
34  }
```

The listing above relied on being able to compute the sine of the angle made between three points. The code for this is below.

```
Listing 8.8: Sine of Angle Between Points
1  double sine_of_angle(point a, point b, point c) {
2    auto bottom = unit_vector(b - a);
3    auto top = unit_vector(c - b);
4    return top.x * bottom.y - top.y * bottom.x;
5  }
```

Note that above we have used the identity that $\vec{a} \times \vec{b} = |\vec{a}| \cdot |\vec{b}| \sin\theta$.

8.6 A point in a polygon

And with that we are done. The listing below finds the area of a polygon given a point from which to triangulate.

```
Listing 8.9: Area of a Polygon
1  double area(const polygon& p, const point& d) {
2    double sum = 0.0;
3    for (size_t i = 0; i < p.size(); ++i) {
4      triangle t(p[i],
5                 p[(i+1) % p.size()],
6                 d);
7      sum += area(t);
8    }
9    return sum;
10 }
```

The final algorithm to determine if a point is in the interior of a polygon is presented in the listing below.

Listing 8.10: Point in a Polygon

```
1  bool point_in_polygon(const polygon& p,
2                         const point& d) {
3    polygon hull = convex_hull(p);
4    point interior_point = center(hull);
5    double polygon_area = area(hull, interior_point);
6    double triangulation_area = area(hull, d);
7    return
8      std::abs(triangulation_area - polygon_area)
9        < epsilon;
10 }
```

Its brevity belies the complexity we encountered in generalizing from triangles to convex polygons.

Chapter 9

Classic String Problems

Operations on strings are ubiquitous in programming problems. After all, much of computation is done to format, modify, and manipulate text. Because of the implementation of strings as null terminated character arrays in C, knowing how to handle string operations is deeply tied with knowing how to handle pointer operations. And pointer operations have always made for interesting programming problems.

Classic questions of string manipulation usually take three forms. There easiest are standard operations, such as ASCII to integer conversion and string tokenization. These are simple questions, although they take some thought on first attempt. Next there is simple parsing and equivalence checking. Then there will be in place modifications of strings, including the most famous Microsoft interview question to reverse the words of a string. Finally, there are more complex string operations such as parsing and regular expression matching.

As C/C++ has advanced, there are fewer reasons to know how to handle and manipulate C style strings. Much of the burdens of string manipulation are alleviated by using the standard string class and avoiding the cstring library. However, technical interviews are interested in seeing how you solve a tractable problems in the limits defined by the interview. To help think along these lines, all the programming problems in this section will consider only C style string. This will force some redundancy, such as checking input parameters for the `nullptr` and bounds checking. However, in the end we will have a complete understanding of what our basic string operations and their cost.

In the next section, we look at implementations of basic string operations. Next, we looks at types of string equivalence, and consider class equivalence by constructing a simple regular expression parser. We proceed to review some more common string manipulations, and conclude solving the problem of paragraph justification.

9.1   Standard string procedures

The standard library supports strings through the `string.h` library. These procedures are for the most part simple, and each provides a simple exercise. In this section, we look at a number of these functions. Note that this section should be largely review material, and considered preparation for the sections that follow.

9.1.1   `strlen`

The string length function is an extremely simple api which is asked too commonly. The only point of interest is that the standard does not specify what to do if the input is the null pointer. Often the answer is simply to return a sentinel value of -1.

Listing 9.1: `strlen`

```
1  size_t strlen(const char* str) {
2    if (!str) return -1;
3    const char* p = str;
4    while(*p++);
5    return p - str - 1;
6  }
```

When solving this programming problem, be sure to check the error conditions. Above it is whether or not the parameter is `nullptr`. Note that there is no getting around a temporary variable to track length. In the listing above, we use pointer arithmetic. To review, a properly formatted input is null terminated. The algorithm iterates through each position in the character array until the null character is found, and returns the difference of the current pointer and the pointer to the head of the string. This difference is the number of bytes between the two pointers.

Note this implementation is not safe. If the string is malformed, the program may terminate in a bus error. This is a trait of most legacy string problems of which everyone should be aware. A safer implementation would take a maximum value in order to avoid an unterminated string causing the method to access random data. That value could be used as a counter.

9.1.2 `strcpy`

Only slightly more complicated is the `strcpy` api. Similar questions take the forms of `memcpy` or `memmove`. The standard requires that the parameters specify a source and destination. The `memcpy` api also requires the length of the sub-array to copy from the source to the destination. For `strcpy` we will find use of this signature in the sequel and implement the `memcpy` signature here.

Aside from a single matter, the problem is straightforward. One needs to handle the character read, write, and indexing properly. The programming problem often requires a guarantee that at termination the output buffer contains the value provided by the input buffer. The corner case is then determining if there is overlapping memory locations.

The following listing handles this case.

Listing 9.2: `strcpy`

```
1  void strcpy(char* destination,
2               const char* source, int len) {
3    if (destination == source) return;
4    if (!source || !destination) return;
5    if (source < destination
6        && destination < (source + len)) {
7      while(len--) *(destination+len)=*(source+len);
8    } else {
9      while(len--) *destination++ = *source++;
10   }
11 }
```

Notice we do not need to determine if there is overlap, but only if there is possible overlap. If we proceed in the memory copy from left to right, then overlap can occur only if the head of the output buffer is between the head and tail of the input buffer. If it is, it is sufficient to copy from right to left to avoid invaliding the output buffer. This is because the buffers are contiguous. If this condition does not hold, we require a different solution.

9.1.3 `strtok`

The final standard function we examine in this section is `strtok`. This method is used to extract sub-arrays from a string given a set of tokens from which to split.

We first reconstruct the standard implementation. The standard requires the return of a pointer to the start of the first token in the string. The token is separated from the remainder of the string by inserting the null character at the beginning of the next split. When null string is provided as a parameter, the next token in the initial string is returned. When null is finally returned by this function, enumeration is complete.

Note that the input string is modified at termination.

Listing 9.3: strtok

```
1  char* strtok(char* str, const char* delim) {
2    static char* next_str = nullptr;
3    if (!delim) return nullptr;
4    if (str) {
5      next_str = str;
6    }
7    if (!next_str || !*next_str) return nullptr;
8    auto span = strcspn(next_str, delim);
9    while (!span && *next_str) {
10     ++next_str;
11     span = strcspn(next_str, delim);
12   }
13   if (next_str && *next_str) {
14     str = next_str;
15     next_str += std::min(span+1,strlen(next_str));
16     str[span] = '\0';
17   }
18   return str;
19 }
```

Clearly, the use of static variables shows that this implementation is not thread safe. While it is compatible with the functionality provided by the standard library, it is not something that would be allowed through a code review. Amongst its other shortcomings is that it modifies the input and requires the caller to return the input to its previous form if necessary.

A better implementation is to implement a split function using a container class to hold the extracted sub-arrays of the string. This can be done by mimicking the scan above, but copying tokenized substrings into a temporary array of buffers. In the listing below, we use the stl containers to avoid explicit memory allocation.

Listing 9.4: `split`

```cpp
std::vector<std::string> split(
    const std::string& str,
    const std::string& delim) {
  std::vector<std::string> tokens;
  size_t begin = 0;
  size_t end = 0;
  while (end < str.length()) {
    while (end < str.length() &&
      (!delim.length() ||
      (delim.find(str[end])==std::string::npos))){
      end++;
    }
    auto len = end - begin;
    if (len > 0) {
      tokens.push_back(std::string(str,begin,len));
    }
    begin = ++end;
  }
  return tokens;
}
```

Notice, that not only is the `split` method safer, but it is also simpler. We only need scan between any two delimitating characters and copy the internal strings. However, the memory allocation for the buffers is often too expensive to use this approach in an inner loop.

9.2   String equivalence

There are many types of string equivalence that can be considered aside from simple character-by-character string comparison. For instance, two strings are rotationally equivalent if they are simple shifts of each other. Two strings are anagrams if they have the same character composition, or the same character set and frequency of occurrence. Two strings can also be considered part of a similarity class if they match the same regular expression.

In this section, we look at all of these types of equivalence, beginning with the standard library function `strcmp`.

9.2.1 `strcmp`

Standard string comparison is a simple to implement standard library method. Two strings are equivalent only if they have the same composition at every position. The standard requires that 0 be returned if the parameters are equivalent. Else, a negative or positive value is returned depending on if the first parameter is lexicographically lower than the second.

Listing 9.5: `strcmp`

```
int strcmp(const char * str1, const char * str2) {
  if (!str1 && !str2) return 0;
  if (!str) return -1;
  if (!str2) return 1;
  while (*str1 && *str2) {
    auto cmp = *str1++ - *str2++;
    if (cmp) return cmp;
  }
  return *str1 - *str2;
}
```

Above we take the difference of ASCII values to determine character equality.

As with other standard methods, the only thing to watch for is bounds checking and undefined behavior. In many implementations, if one parameter is a `nullptr` the function will crash. However, for convenience we suppose that the `nullptr` is the lexicographically smallest C style string.

9.2.2 Rotational equivalence

In the next programming problem, we want to determine if two strings are rotationally equivalent. Two strings are rotationally equivalent if one is formed from the other by shifting the string one direction and wrapping the overflow back around onto the buffer. For instance "abcde" shifted to the right by three characters results "cdeab".

A naive algorithm takes it in turn to consider every possible shift. There is one shift for each integer value less than the length of the string. For each shift, we see if the suffix from that position of the first string matches the prefix of the second as well as if the suffix of the second string matches the prefix of the first. If they do, we have found the shift value.

```
Listing 9.6: Rotationally Equivalent
 1  bool rot_equiv(const char* a, const char* b) {
 2    if (a == b) return true;
 3    if (!a || !b) return false;
 4    if (strlen(a) != strlen(b)) return false;
 5    auto alen = strlen(a);
 6    for (int rot = 0; rot < alen; ++rot) {
 7      if (!strncmp(a, b + rot, alen - rot) &&
 8          !strncmp(a + alen - rot, b, rot))
 9        return true;
10    }
11    return false;
12  }
```

Above we use strncmp to check the prefix and suffix match for each possible shift of the first parameter.

The naive implementation above determines rotation equivalence in quadratic time. The reason is that every shift of the first parameter is checked against the second.

A nice trick that can provide not only a faster, but also a simpler solution. Suppose we construct a new string by appending the second parameter to itself. If the second parameter is a rotation of the first, then this new string must have the first as two substrings. When considered with wrap around at most one of those substrings will not be contiguous. Hence, the first will be a contiguous sub-array of the new string. In addition, there is support for substring search in the standard library.

Listing 9.7: Simple Rotationally Equivalent

```
1  bool rot_equiv(const char* a, const char* b) {
2      if (a == b) return true;
3      if (!a || !b) return false;
4      if (strlen(a) != strlen(b)) return false;
5      std::string b2 = b;
6      b2 += b;
7      return nullptr != strstr(b2.c_str(), a);
8  }
```

Above, we used `std::string` to avoid memory allocation for the string copy. The substring search can occur in constant time, as we will see in a future section. So not only is the above algorithm linear, it also avoids indexing problems.

9.2.3 Anagrams

Recall that anagrams are words and sentences formed from permuting another word or sentence. For instance "army" and "mary" are anagrams. Anagrams often do not consider white space or capitalization, for instance "San Diego" and "agonised". Considering only composition of characters without relational position in the string, anagrams form an equivalence class of strings.

Determining if two strings are anagrams can be done very quickly in a naive implementation. The idea is that only the count of each character need be determined. These counts can be easily tracked in a histogram indexed by characters.

Listing 9.8: Determine if Two Strings are Anagrams

```cpp
bool anagrams(const char* a, const char* b) {
  if (!a && !b) return true;
  if (!a || !b) return false;
  std::array<int, 128> histogram = {};
  while (*a) {
    histogram[*a++] += 1;
  }
  while (*b) {
    histogram[*b++] -= 1;
  }
  for (auto& entry: histogram) {
    if (entry) return false;
  }
  return true;
}
```

The solution above works well for ASCII characters since there are only 128 of them to consider. However, for multi-byte character sets the histogram may be too large. A simple modification may attempt to use a hash table. However, it is effective to sort the characters of the string and determining if they are equivalent.

Listing 9.9: Determine if Two Strings are Anagrams By Sorting

```cpp
bool anagrams(const char* a, const char* b) {
  if (!a && !b) return true;
  if (!a || !b) return false;
  std::string acopy(a);
  std::string bcopy(b);
  std::sort(acopy.begin(), acopy.end());
  std::sort(bcopy.begin(), bcopy.end());
  return acopy == bcopy;
}
```

This approach can be used to classify large sets of strings into the equivalence classes determined by the anagram relation by mapping every string to a single canonical representative of the class.

9.2.4 Regular expressions

Pattern matching is becoming a commonly asked problem. Common string editing problems require iteration and careful state tracking. However, pattern matching requires clever use of recursion or finite automata. This is a large step up in complexity.

In the following, we consider the decision problem of a string being accepted by an expression. Note that regular expressions are often used to find some substring that matches an expression. With this problem we will implement a solution that decides whether or not the expression matches entirely, but can be generalized.

Consider implementing a regular expression matcher with a simplified grammar. The simplest interesting grammar allows the matching of alphanumeric character as well as the ".*" wildcard. Recall that the "." wildcard allows a match of any character in its location, and the "*" modifier specifies that zero or more of the preceding character is allowed.

We consider some examples. With these rules the pattern "abc" matches only itself. The pattern "ab.c" matches any four character string with the prefix "ab" and the suffix "c". The pattern with the multiple wildcard "ab*c" matches any string with a prefix "a" that terminates in "c" after zero or more repetitions of "b". Finally the pattern "a.*c" matches any string that begins with an "a" and ends with "c".

The following recursive decent parser solves this programming problem.

Listing 9.10: match

```
1  bool match(const char* str, const char* expr) {
2    if (*str == '\0' && *expr == '\0') return true;
3    if (*str == '\0' && *(expr+1) != '*')
4      return false;
5    if (*expr == '\0') return false;
6    if (*(expr+1) != '*') {
7      if (*expr != '.' && *str != *expr)
8        return false;
9      return match(str + 1, expr + 1);
10   }
11   if (match(str, expr + 2)) return true;
12   if (*str == '\0') return false;
13   if (*expr != '.' && *str != *expr) return false;
14   return match(str + 1, expr);
15 }
```

The base case is that either the expression is empty or the string is empty but the expression is a wild card. We are careful to add this case since ".*" accepts an empty string. When the expression token being considered is not the wildcard, we must decide if we match a single character or are attempting to match a repeated pattern. Finally, we match the next single character against the wildcard and increment either the string, the expression, or both. In any case, the first mismatch character signals failure.

There are many possible branches in the listing, and it is worthwhile to walk through the examples given to understand how it operates.

9.3   String editing

String editing refers to modifying a string buffer to accomplish simple text tasks. Programming problems in string editing operate on either words or sequences of words. For instance, a simple problem on a word is reversing the characters from left to right to right to left. A more complex problem that builds on the first is reversing the words in a sequence.

String editing is often straightforward and does not require a sequence of tricks or critical insights. However, difficulty is increased when an in place solution is required.

In this section, we look at three string editing programming problems. These are removing duplicate characters, reversing the words in a substring, and justification of a sequence.

9.3.1 Remove duplicate characters

We begin with the programming problem of removing duplicate characters from a string. The api unique requires that the relative position of characters is kept, but every duplicate character is removed.

The listing below gives a straightforward solution.

Listing 9.11: unique

```
1  void unique(char* str) {
2      std::vector<bool> seen(128);
3      char* trailing = str;
4      do {
5          size_t char_value = (size_t) *str;
6          if (seen[char_value]) continue;
7          seen[char_value] = true;
8          if (trailing != str) {
9              *trailing = *str;
10         }
11         ++trailing;
12     } while(*str++);
13     return;
14 }
```

This problem is simplified by constraining the input to ASCII characters. For that we need only a simple lookup to determine if a character has previously been encountered. To do so, we need a bit array of length 128. We maintain a trailing write pointer, and a forward head pointer. Whenever a duplicate character is encountered, we increment the head pointer. When a character is first encountered, it is written to the trailing pointer. Notice that the read ends after the terminating null character has been seen for the first time, ensuring that the modified string is properly terminated.

9.3.2　Reverse the characters of a string

The next problem in string editing is a utility method to reverse the characters of a word. The problem is solved in a straight forward manner by maintaining a head and tail pointer, and terminating when they cross.

Listing 9.12: Reverse string

```
1  void reverse(char* str, int len) {
2    for (int index = 0; index < len / 2; ++index) {
3      str[index] ^= str[len - 1 - index];
4      str[len - 1 - index] ^= str[index];
5      str[index] ^= str[len - 1 - index];
6    }
7  }
```

The listing above avoids the temporary variable usually used in reversing the string by exploiting the Boolean exclusive-or operator to the effect that $b\char`^a\char`^b = a$. However, there is little advantage to this trick, as the temporary is a fast to access stack variable and in either case the swap requires three reads and three writes. Even so it is still worthwhile to know.

We will use this function in the problem below.

9.3.3　Reverse the words in a sentence

Reversing the order in which words appear has some use in practice. For instance to reverse a sorted array of tokens. However, this problem is mostly known for being a common interview question amongst C/C++ programmers and is often asked during Microsoft interviews.

The problem at hand is given a string of whitespace delimitated tokens, reverse the order of the tokens in the string without reversing the characters in the tokens. A first attempt is to swap words in whole, but it is quickly understood that this approach is unwieldy.

The simplifying trick is to use the reverse string function developed above as a subroutine in the solution.

Listing 9.13: Reverse Word Order

```
1  void reverse(char* str) {
2    if (!str || !strlen(str)) return;
3    char* trailing = str;
4    while (*trailing) {
5      while (isspace(*trailing) && *trailing) ++trailing;
6      char* forward = trailing;
7      while (!isspace(*forward) && *forward) ++forward;
8      reverse(trailing, forward-trailing);
9      trailing = forward;
10   }
11   reverse(str, strlen(str));
12 }
```

In effect, two passes of the string are made. The first reverses the characters of each token. After the entire is string is reversed, the tokens are in their original form. This method is much cleaner than attempting maintain a proper stack of write and read values and cheaper than splitting a string into constituent tokens and rewriting them back to the buffer.

9.3.4 Justify a paragraph

Our final string editing problem is that of justifying a paragraph. Commonly used in typography, justification is a string formatting process that attempts to equalize the white space between the tokens within a line. There are many kinds of justification. Total justification aligns both the left and right most characters with the column borders.

To begin, consider justifying a single line. To begin we need a routine to count the number of words in a line. To keep matters simple, we will suppose that the input has tokens separated by only spaces.

Listing 9.14: Count Words For Justification

```cpp
std::pair<size_t, size_t> counts(const char* str) {
  size_t tokens = 0, characters = 0;
  while (*str) {
    while (isspace(*str)) ++str;
    if (*str) ++tokens;
    while (*str && !isspace(*str++)) {
      characters++;
    }
  }
  return std::make_pair(tokens, characters);
}
```

We first count the number of tokens and the number of non-whitespace characters. The difference between this number and the line size is the total number of whitespace characters that must be distributed between tokens. If there are n tokens and m whitespace characters, we must distribute $m/(n-1)$ whitespace characters between each token.

The whitespace is then distributed evenly between every word break within a line. When the whitespace cannot be evenly distributed between word breaks, we choose to place more whitespace on the former word breaks.

Listing 9.15: Justify a Line

```
1  void justify(char* str) {
2    auto len = strlen(str);
3    auto count = counts(str);
4    if (count.first > 1) {
5      auto seps = count.first - 1;
6      auto spaces = (len - count.second) / seps;
7      auto extras = (len - count.second) % seps;
8      char* write = str + len - 1;
9      char* read = write;
10     while (read > str) {
11       while (isspace(*read) && str!=read) --read;
12       while (!isspace(*read) && write >= str) {
13         *write-- = *read--;
14       }
15       for(size_t i=0;i<spaces && write>=str; ++i){
16         *write-- = ' ';
17       }
18       if (extras) {
19         *write-- = ' ';
20         --extras;
21       }
22     }
23   }
24 }
```

We can use the routine above to justifying a paragraph. However, in doing so we will need to prepare the lines of a paragraph for display. The simplest way to do this is to use a greedy algorithm to choose the approximate best splits.

A greedy algorithm is one that attempts to take the best subset possible when first encountered to avoid the complexity of backtracking. Under specific conditions, a greedy algorithm will always result in the optimal solution. And even if those conditions are not met a greedy algorithm usually still results in an excellent approximation.

For justification, we attempt to fill a line with as many words as possible without breaking words. When addition of a word would spill over to the next line, we insert spaces to fill out the line to the specified length and a line break character and continue.

The following listing does this by first determining line breaks, and then padding every line break with additional whitespace to fill the line. Line breaks are found by search for the first whitespace character at a line boundary. When this is found, we store it as line break point. The next search then starts from the maximum line break from this offset. The second loop then works in reverse, moving the string segments determined above to the line offset and padding whitespace.

```
 1  void prepare_to_justify(char* buf,
 2                               size_t len) {
 3    std::stack<char*> breaks;
 4    auto slen = strlen(buf);
 5    auto prev = 0;
 6    while (prev + len <= slen) {
 7      auto offset = prev + len - 1;
 8      while (prev < offset && !isspace(buf[offset]))
 9        --offset;
10      if (prev == offset) offset = prev + len - 1;
11      if (isspace(buf[offset])) ++offset;
12      breaks.push(buf + offset);
13      prev = offset;
14    }
15    char* prev_br = nullptr;
16    while (!breaks.empty()) {
17      auto src = breaks.top();
18      auto move_pos = buf + breaks.size() * len;
19      auto dist = !prev_br ?
20        strlen(src) :
21        std::min<size_t>(len - 1, prev_br - src);
22      strcpy(move_pos, src, dist);
23      if (prev_br)
24        memset(move_pos + dist, ' ', len-dist-1);
25      else move_pos[dist] = '\0';
26      *(move_pos-1) = '\n';
27      breaks.pop();
28      prev_br = src;
29    }
30    if (prev_br && (prev_br-buf) < len)
31      memset(prev_br, ' ', len-(prev_br-buf)-1);
32  }
```

The listing above is straightforward, but the use of pointer manipulation makes is delicate. While it is presented as an in place operation, we have assumed that the buffer is large enough to hold as many lines as needed.

After pre-processing, we justify a paragraph for display by then calling the line justification algorithm on every line identified above. With whitespace padding, this is much simplified.

Listing 9.17: Justify a Paragraph

```cpp
void justify_paragraph(char* str, size_t len) {
  prepare_to_justify(str, len);
  auto slen = strlen(str);
  for (auto offset=0; offset<slen; offset += len){
    auto num = std::min(len - 1, slen - offset);
    auto c = (str + offset)[num];
    (str + offset)[num] = '\0';
    justify(str + offset);
    (str + offset)[num] = c;
  }
}
```

The greedy algorithm for justification is used in many text processing packages because it is linear time and easy to implement. There are other solutions to this problem as well, such as the Knuth-Plass line breaking algorithm. That algorithm attempts to minimize the difference of the square of additional whitespace in lines. It can be implemented in linear time, but with much greater complexity than is required for the greedy approach. Even today there is no standard in modern text processing software, with some using greedy and others using more sophisticated algorithms.

Chapter 10

Substring Search

The problem of substring search is to determine when given two strings whether one is a substring of the other. In this problem, the pattern is the substring to be found in the text. However, the study of this problem has developed deep algorithms.

Substring search comes up quite often in discussion of programming problems, but an optimal solution is usually not required. What is required is a naive solution that is correct. What is hoped for is the ability to recognize the asymptotic run time of the naive solution followed by knowledgeable discussion about techniques to speed up this decision problem.

We begin this section with the naive quadratic solution. We then develop two optimal solutions, first the Knuth-Morris-Pratt algorithm and second the industry standard Boyer-Moore algorithm. We conclude with a randomized solution developed by Rabin and Karp, and note other uses for the randomized technique developed. The goal of this chapter is to review the techniques for optimal substring matching, understand the insights required, and discuss their implementation.

10.1 Quadratic substring search

The obvious approach to substring match is to check in sequence whether any character of the text is the beginning of the pattern. This naive substring search requires only proper iterator manipulation and bounds checking. At every location, a complete comparison of the text is done against the pattern until a mismatch is located.

Listing 10.1: Quadratic Substring Search

```
 1  size_t find(const std::string& str,
 2              const std::string& sub) {
 3    for (auto i = 0;
 4         i + sub.length() < str.length() + 1;
 5         ++i) {
 6      auto matching = true;
 7      for (auto j = 0;
 8           j < sub.length() && matching;
 9           ++j) {
10        if (str[i+j] != sub[j]) {
11          matching = false;
12        }
13      }
14      if (matching) return i;
15    }
16    return sub.empty() ? 0 : std::string::npos;
17  }
```

Suppose that the text S is of size m and the pattern T is of size n. For each character s of S, the pattern is aligned at s and every character from this offset is compared between the two strings. It is obvious that such a straightforward implementation has run time $O(mn)$, which is quadratic.

There are some well known attempts to speed up this approach. For instance attempting suffix match instead of prefix match. Another involves only checking the first $m - n$ characters and matching 64 bits at a time. However, without further insight these approaches do not change the asymptotic run time. These attempts lack a mechanism to reuse the information gathered during the substring check of the prefix. This deficiency was first overcome by Donald Knuth and Vaughan Pratt in 1974, and published by Knuth, Morris, and Pratt in 1977.

10.2   Knuth-Morris-Pratt substring search

Observe that the naive algorithm can be viewed as sliding a window across the search string. If the search string window completely aligns with the pattern, we are done. Otherwise, the window alignment is incremented and start over. If we can avoid starting over, then we can hope to affect a speed up. This is the idea of the Knuth-Morris-Pratt algorithm.

The algorithm builds a fallback table that allows the window to be incremented with each comparison. This is done by pre-searching the pattern, and determining the rightmost alignment that can be considered given a match of the prefix pattern. This is done by building a jump table.

To understand the approach, study the listing below.

Listing 10.2: Knuth-Morris-Pratt Table Creation

```
 1  void build_kmp_table(const std::string& sub,
 2                        std::vector<int>* table) {
 3    auto pos = 2;
 4    auto fallback_pos = 0;
 5    if (table->size() < 2) table->resize(2);
 6    (*table)[0] = -1;
 7    (*table)[1] = 0;
 8    for (auto pos = 2, fallback_pos = 0;
 9         pos < sub.length();
10         ++pos) {
11      while (sub[pos] != sub[fallback_pos]
12             && fallback_pos > 0) {
13        fallback_pos = (*table)[fallback_pos];
14      }
15      if (sub[pos] == sub[fallback_pos]) {
16        (*table)[pos] = ++fallback_pos;
17        continue;
18      }
19      (*table)[pos] = 0;
20    }
21  }
```

The listing builds up the fallback table F in linear time. At index j, the fallback table contains the right most position k preceding

j such that the sub-array ending at $t[j]$ matches the prefix of T of length k. For instance, consider the sting *abac*. If substring matching fails at $t[3] = c$, then if we fall back to $t[1] = b$ instead of all the way to index 0.

With this lookup table, the evaluation of substring match proceeds as follows. Two indexes are maintained. The index i tracks the alignment of the text and pattern. The index j tracks an index of the pattern. For each character in the string, if that character matches then both indexes are incremented. In the event of the mismatch $s[i + j] \neq t[j]$, then the text alignment falls back to $j = f[j]$. If $j \geq 0$, we compare $s[i + j]$ and $t[j]$. Otherwise, we slide the pattern forward by i and iterate. This algorithm is implemented in the listing below.

Listing 10.3: Knuth-Morris-Pratt Substring Search

```
 1  size_t find(const std::string& str,
 2                const std::string& sub) {
 3    std::vector<int> table(sub.length());
 4    build_kmp_table(sub, &table);
 5    auto str_pos = 0;
 6    auto substr_pos = 0;
 7    while (str_pos + substr_pos < str.length() &&
 8           substr_pos < sub.length()) {
 9      if (str[str_pos + substr_pos] ==
10          sub[substr_pos]) {
11        if (substr_pos == sub.length() - 1) {
12          return str_pos;
13        }
14        ++substr_pos;
15        continue;
16      }
17      str_pos += substr_pos - table[substr_pos];
18      if (table[substr_pos] > -1) {
19        substr_pos = table[substr_pos];
20      } else substr_pos = 0;
21    }
22    return sub.empty() ? 0 : std::string::npos;
23  }
```

The running time of this algorithm can be bounded above by

observing how many times j can be incremented and decremented in a scan of the text. The answer is surprisingly only $2m$. The reason is that if j ever falls back, it was because it had been previously incremented. It can only be incremented once for each character of S, and is decremented otherwise. Hence, we see the Knuth-Morris-Pratt substring search algorithm has linear run time with use of the fallback table. Since that table is built in linear time, the entire algorithm is linear in the length of the input.

10.3 Boyer-Moore substring search

The Boyer-Moore substring search algorithm was published in 1977, the same year the Knuth-Morris-Pratt algorithm was published. It is a more detailed algorithm, using suffix matching and relying on two fallback tables. While it has the same asymptotic running time as Knuth-Morris-Pratt, in practice it often speeds up as the pattern length increases. This property has made it an industry standard for benchmarking substring matching.

Boyer-Moore relies on two shift rules to affect linear substring matching. These are the bad character rule and the good suffix rule. Each rule is identified with a jump table that is used in evaluation of a substring match. We discuss each rule below.

The bad character rule defines the shift of alignment on a character mismatch. During matching the algorithm maintains two indexes i and j. Index i is the position in the text that defines the current alignment of the pattern and text. Index j identifies that position in the pattern that the algorithm evaluating. The bad character rule attempts to update i so that $sub[j] == str[i+j]$ when a character mismatch is detected at text position $i+j$ and pattern position j. Hence, for a bad character c not in the pattern there is no such i and we need to update i and j to resume searching one character beyond $i + j$. If c is in the pattern, then we need to shift i over to the right most location of c in the text that has not yet been matched. The shift is to the right most location because we the Boyer-Moore algorithm attempts to compare the pattern to the text from right to left.

The following listing builds a bad character table. The bad character table has length equal to the alphabet size. The function expects the table parameter have default values of -1. For each character in the pattern, the difference between the end of the

pattern and the position is stored. As the table is populated from
left to right, the final jump for character c is equal to the minimum
distance needed to reposition i.

Listing 10.4: Boyer-Moore Bad Character Rule Table Creation

```
1  void make_bad_character_table(
2      const std::string& sub,
3      std::vector<int>* table) {
4    for (auto i = 0; i + 1 < sub.length(); i++) {
5      (*table)[sub[i]] = sub.length() - (i + 1);
6    }
7  }
```

It is clear that this requires a linear scan, and space equal to the
size of the alphabet.

The good suffix rule defines the shift of alignment based on a
partial suffix match. The Boyer-Moore algorithm scans the pattern
from right to left. Hence, if a character mismatch is detected at
pattern position $j - 1$, then the suffix of the pattern has matched
the text from pattern index j to its end. The pattern alignment
should be shifted to match the suffix of the pattern with the next
match to the left of the pattern. In this way, scanning can continue
from the mismatched location in the text.

The following listing builds a good suffix table, and incorporates
some of the intricacies of the algorithm. The good suffix table has
length equal to the pattern. The table is built up in two passes of
the pattern, scanning from right to left then left to right. In the first
pass, the shift stored insures that the best known suffix alignment is
found. That is if k is the best detected prefix of the pattern starts
at j, then the value stored at position k is $m - k + j$. This allows
shifting the alignment so the prefix of the pattern matching the
suffix is shifted passes k. The second pass insures that the minimum
shift is recorded.

```cpp
void make_good_suffix_table(
    const std::string& sub,
    std::vector<int>* table) {
  int m = sub.length();
  table->resize(m+1);
  std::vector<int> z(m + 1);
  int i = m, j = m + 1;
  z[i] = j;
  while (i > 0) {
    while (j <= m && sub[i-1] != sub[j-1]) {
      if ((*table)[j] == 0) (*table)[j] = j - i;
      j = z[j];
    }
    i--; j--;
    z[i] = j;
  }
  j = z[0];
  for (i = 0; i <= m; ++i) {
    if ((*table)[i] == 0) (*table)[i] = j;
    if (i == j) j = z[j];
  }
}
```

It is clear to see that the second loop is a linear scan of the pattern. The first loop is nested, however in the inner loop j falls back to m as in the Knuth-Morris-Pratt algorithm. Hence, the construction time of the good suffix table is again linear.

The use of these tables provides a linear substring match algorithm. Alignment of the pattern is initially at the first character of text. The pattern is then compared against the text from right to left. When a mismatch is detected, the alignment is shifted by the maximum of the bad character rule and the good suffix rule. This evaluation is implemented in the following listing.

Listing 10.6: Boyer-Moore Substring Search

```
1  size_t find(const std::string& str,
2              const std::string& sub) {
3    if (sub.empty()) return 0;
4    std::vector<int> bad_char(1 << 8, -1);
5    std::vector<int> good_suffix(sub.length()+1);
6    make_bad_character_table(sub, &bad_char);
7    make_good_suffix_table(sub, &good_suffix);
8    int i = 0;
9    while (i + sub.length() < str.length() + 1) {
10     int j = sub.length() - 1;
11     while ((str[i + j] == sub[j]) && --j >= 0);
12     if (j < 0) {
13       return i;
14     }
15     i += std::max(bad_char[str[i+j]],
16                   good_suffix[j+1]);
17   }
18   return std::string::npos;
19 }
```

The Boyer-Moore algorithm is complex, but the good suffix rule is not something that should be memorized. Instead note that the idea of suffix matching is a main insight. However, the bad character rule is simple and useful in practice. It is a clever trick that makes studying the Boyer-Moore algorithm worthwhile.

10.4   Rabin-Karp rolling hash

Our final substring matching algorithm is probabilistic in nature and provides linear time guarantees in expectation.

The Rabin-Karp randomized substring search uses the technique of calculating a rolling hash. A rolling hash is a hash function that has two properties. First it is a function of a defined number k parameters, say t_1 to t_k. Second, given a value t_{k+1}, the hash value of the sequence t_2 to t_{k+1} can calculated in constant time. With these two properties, a rolling hash can be calculated in sequence for every alignment of a pattern of length k in time linear in the length of the text.

There are many implementations of a rolling hash. Commonly a rolling hash function is implemented as a polynomial of degree k. To see why, consider the following cubic polynomial $p(x)$.

$$p(x) = a + b \cdot x + c \cdot x^2 + d \cdot x^3$$

Here the choice of x specializes the polynomial. Once specialized, the polynomial can be considered a function of four parameters a, b, c, d. Suppose now that we have a string S of length n. The first hash of this string comes from calculating the polynomial by replacing the coefficients with the values of the first four characters. That is we calculate

$$p(x) = s[1] + s[2] * x + s[3] * x^2 + s[4] * x^3$$

This is a function of S. To calculate the hash of $s[2]$ to $s[5]$, we can update the value by taking three simple steps. First we subtract $s[1]$ from the sum, then divide through by x and add the term $s[4] * x^3$. That is given $p_l(x)$, we have the constant time update equation $p_{l+1} = (p_l - s_l)/x + s_{l+k} * x^3$.

Note that if x is larger than any coefficient, the update rule is vastly simplified. That is $p_l = p_{l-1}/x + s_{l+k} * x^{k-1}$. For alphanumeric characters we would need x to be at least 36. However, in general, such a large value for x is not needed and a more naive update rule is used.

In the implementation below, the rolling hash is updated to calculate the sub-array hash at every alignment. The rolling hash is simplified in that x is taken to be 1. When the rolling hash is equal to the hash of the pattern, a possible matching alignment is found. When a possible match is found, a full substring comparison is attempted to confirm. This is implemented in the listing below.

Listing 10.7: Rabin-Karp Substring Search

```
1  size_t find(const std::string& str,
2              const std::string& sub) {
3    if (sub.empty()) return 0;
4    auto hash = 0;
5    auto update_hash = [&str, &hash] (size_t pos,
6                                      size_t len) {
7      if (0 == pos) {
8        return std::accumulate(str.begin(),
9                               str.begin() + len,
10                              0);
11     }
12     return hash + str[pos-1 + len] - str[pos-1];
13   };
14   auto target = 0;
15   for (auto& c : sub) {
16     target += c;
17   }
18   for (auto pos = 0;
19        pos + sub.length() < str.length() + 1;
20        ++pos) {
21     hash = update_hash(pos, sub.length());
22     if (hash == target
23         && !str.compare(pos, sub.length(), sub)) {
24       return pos;
25     }
26   }
27   return std::string::npos;
28 }
```

The worst case running time of the above algorithm is quadratic, however it is linear in expectation given a good hash function and a random pair of text and pattern.

The rolling hash is an important concept in computer science. A use beyond substring match is document fingerprinting. Suppose we are given a document. Begin iteratively calculating the rolling hash of the document. However, whenever the rolling hash equals 0 store the location that this happens in the document. This list of zero crossings determines a document fingerprint. This fingerprinting technique allows web crawlers to know when a document has been updated, and which parts of the document need be re-indexed, without having to do complex substring matching or entire document comparison.

Chapter 11

Parsing

Parsing is the computational task of constructing a data structure from a sequence of tokens. Simple parsing is required to recognize and read roman numerals, complex parsing occurs when we compile a module or interpret a package.

Parsing and interpretation are intricately tied together. Many complex systems combine the two operations. In this chapter, we study programming problems related to the parsing of numeric expressions. We begin with the conversion of strings to values. This will form the basis of our lexical parsing system. We then recall the simplistic stack based parsing required to interpret postfix notation. Next, we review the Dijkstra's shunting yard algorithm to convert infix to postfix notation.

The path from numerical parsing to infix to postfix conversion can be long, and while it provides a satisfying path of discovery, it is worth reviewing how to accomplish infix expression evaluation directly. We conclude by developing a simple infix parser that respects operator precedence.

11.1   Simple numerical parsing

In order to parse complex expressions, we need to parse the values that are being operated on. In this subsection, we look at the classic problem of converting an ASCII string to either an integer value or a decimal value. These sub-routines will be used throughout the remainder of this chapter, and provide a warm up exercise to this section.

11.1.1 `ASCII` to integer value

Implementing the standard library function `atoi` has been a standard gating question for many years. The question is generally posed with the standard function declaration which converse a C style string to an integer value. As such, it requires parsing an input character array and returning the signed integer value it represents.

While there are many ways to approach this problem, the simplest approach is to parse the string from left to right.

Listing 11.1: `ASCII` String To Integer

```
1   int atoi(const char* str) {
2     int retval = 0;
3     if (!str || !*str) return retval;
4     auto mult = (*str == '-') ? -1 : 1;
5     if (mult == -1) ++str;
6     while ('0' <= *str && *str <= '9') {
7       retval = retval * 10 + *str++ - '0';
8     }
9     return mult * retval;
10  }
```

The main loop traverses the string visiting each character from left to right. During this processing, we keep a running total. For each character, this total is first multiplied by 10. This has the effect of shifting each numeral one place left. Afterward value represented by the current character is added to the value.

Observe that to correctly implement this process there are only two special cases to watch for. These are negative values and the expected behavior upon reaching the fist non-numeric value. To be of use in the future, our parser will return the value of the first integral value parsed or 0 if none are found. Note that it is just a correct to throw on invalid input.

11.1.2 `ASCII` to decimal value

Our second simple numeric parsing is the implementation of the standard library function `atof`. This api is made more difficult because the decimal point adds complexity. In the following, we parse a decimal expression, but we do not parse scientific notation.

Listing 11.2: ASCII String To Double

```
1   float atof(const char* str) {
2     float retval = 0.0;
3     float decimal = 0.0;
4     if (!str || !*str) return retval;
5     auto mult = (*str == '-') ? -1.0 : 1.0;
6     if (mult == -1.0) ++str;
7     retval = atoi(str);
8     for(; '0' <= *str && *str <= '9'; ++str);
9     if (*str && *str++ == '.') {
10      decimal = atoi(str);
11      if (decimal) {
12        decimal /= pow(10, ceil(log10(decimal)));
13      }
14    }
15    return mult * (retval + decimal);
16  }
```

For convenience, the solution above re-uses the `atoi` procedure we developed before. Note that our implementation returned the first integer available for parsing and terminated when a non-integer character was encountered. It is applied to both the characteristic and the mantissa of the decimal expression. After the characteristic is parsed, the string pointer is moved passed the decimal and the mantissa is parsed. In order to express the mantissa as fraction we then divide it by the next power of 10 greater or equal to the value returned by parsing.

This seems simpler than converting `ASCII` to integers. However, it may seem so only because call to the sub-procedure has simplified the code.

11.2   Complex arithmetic expressions

Our next programming problems begin to deal with the parsing of complex arithmetic expressions. Arithmetic expressions are sequences of numbers and operators that specify a calculation. The numbers we will constrain to integers. The arithmetic operators we consider are $+, -, *, /$. Operator precedence must be respected, and sub expressions can be identified by using parenthesis.

In the following sections, we will look at problems of evaluating simplified arithmetic expressions. Numbers will be constrained to be a single decimal digit. Further we will only consider the $+$ and $*$ operations. This will simplify the listings of algorithms, but as we still have operator precedence we will lose no generality.

We first look at parsing expressions in postfix notation, and then use this parser to evaluate expressions in the more familiar infix notation.

11.2.1   Postfix notation

Postfix notation is also referred to as Reverse Polish Notation or RPN. In postfix notation, an arithmetic operation is encoded so that both operands immediately precede any arithmetic operation. As we shall see this simplifies parsing of postfix expressions.

Postfix notation does not require parenthesis to group sub-expressions. Further operator precedence is encoded into the order in which operators appear in an expression. For instance, the infix expression $1 + 2 * 3$ must be written in postfix as $2\ 3 * 1 +$ to evaluate the product prior to the sum

In parsing a postfix expression, we use a stack of values. We begin from the left hand side and evaluate the tokens from left to right. When a number is identified, its value is pushed on to a stack. When an operator is identified, it is applied to the top two values on the stack. The result of each operation is then pushed on to the stack. At completion of the parse, the stack should be of depth one containing the value of the expression.

This parsing scheme developed in the listing below.

Listing 11.3: Postfix Expression

```
int evaluate(const char* expr) {
    std::stack<int> vals;
    for (expr; *expr; ++expr) {
        switch (*expr) {
            case '+': {
                int lhs = vals.top(); vals.pop();
                int rhs = vals.top(); vals.pop();
                vals.push(lhs + rhs);
                break;
            }
            case '*': {
                int lhs = vals.top(); vals.pop();
                int rhs = vals.top(); vals.pop();
                vals.push(lhs * rhs);
                break;
            }
            default:
                vals.push(*expr - '0');
                break;
        }
    }
    return vals.top();
}
```

It is worth noting that our simplified expressions do not have white space delimitating terms of the expression. This can be easily rectified by splitting text on whitespace and evaluating each token.

Handling subtraction and division are as simple as adding new case statements to the listing below. However, to support negative numbers as operands one needs to be able to distinguish when a dash refers to subtraction or to negation. A simple method to avoid ambiguity is to require whitespace separation of tokens. Otherwise, disambiguation requires keeping track of a parse tree.

11.2.2 Infix expression conversion

Arithmetic is usually written in infix notation. In postfix notation, operands are succeeded by their operators directly so placement directs the order of computation. In infix notation, operator precedence over-rides the placement of operands and operators in the expression. Because of this, parentheses are required to correctly write expressions, and this must be handled in parsing.

Aware of the simplicity of parsing postfix arithmetic expressions, it is reasonable to approach parsing an infix expression with the goal of first converting it to postfix. And by rediscovering Dijkstra's shunting yard algorithm this goal can be accomplished.

The idea of the algorithm is to use two data structures. The first is the output buffer, and the second is a stack that holds operators. In the listing below, we assume that the output buffer rpn is at least as large as the input.

During parsing, when values are encountered they are shunted directly to the output. Operators are shunted to either the output or the stack depending on their precedence and placement. Whenever precedence allows, operators are popped off the stack and in to place in the postfix expression.

Listing 11.4: Convert Numeric Expression To Postfix

```cpp
void infix_2_postfix(const char* expr, char* rpn) {
  std::stack<char> ops;
  for (expr; expr && *expr; ++expr) {
    switch(*expr) {
      case '(':
        ops.push('(');
        break;
      case ')':
        while ('(' != ops.top()) {
          *rpn++ = ops.top(); ops.pop();
        }
        ops.pop();
        break;
      case '*':
        if (ops.empty() || '(' == ops.top()) {
          ops.push('*');
          break;
        }
        *rpn++ = '*';
        break;
      case '+':
        if (ops.empty() ||
            ('('==ops.top() && '*'!=ops.top())) {
          ops.push('+');
          break;
        }
        while(!ops.empty()
              && '(' != ops.top()
              && '*' == ops.top()) {
          *rpn++ = ops.top(); ops.pop();
        }
        ops.push('+');
        break;
      default:
        *rpn++ = *expr;
        break;
    }
  }
  while (!ops.empty()){
    *rpn++ = ops.top(); ops.pop();
  }
  *rpn = '\0';
}
```

This algorithm can be recreated by remembering a few simple cases. Namely, that when the first operator is encountered at most one operand has been seen, so a single pass needs the operator stack. Secondly every parenthetical expression can be evaluated when its closing is found. Finally, higher precedence means that an operator can be immediately applied while lower precedence means an operator should be shunted to the stack. These few cases can be recalled with the example of parsing "(1+2)*3+4*5"

11.2.3   Infix expression interpreter

We conclude with the development of a direct infix expression parser. To directly parse an infix expression, we can notice that at any time an operator is shunted onto the output buffer above, it is possible to evaluate the suffix of the output buffer. Using this observation, our direct parser combines the shunting algorithm and the postfix parser.

The postfix parser required a stack of operands. The shunting algorithm required a stack of operators. In the following, we will find that we need to maintain each of these stacks as well.

In the operation stack, we will store pointers to functions that operate on the values. Every operation takes two values and returns a third. The type of these function pointers is defined below.

Listing 11.5: Operation Definition

```
1  typedef int (*operation)(int,int);
```

The operations under consideration are addition and multiplication. However, it will be convenient to define a parenthetical operation. This operation will have no affect on values, but will serve as a stop marker during stack inspection. These three operations are declared in the listing below.

Listing 11.6: Operations for Infix Parsing

```
1  int plus(int x, int y) { return x + y; }
2  int times(int x, int y) { return x * y; }
3  operation paren = nullptr;
```

In the full solution below, we will have use for the following helper function to affect an operation on the top two values in the value stack. Its only purpose is to simplify the code by removing common lines.

Listing 11.7: Operation Evaluation

```
1  void apply_top(std::stack<operation>* ops,
2                 std::stack<int>* vals) {
3    int lhs = vals->top(); vals->pop();
4    int rhs = vals->top(); vals->pop();
5    vals->push(ops->top()(lhs, rhs));
6    ops->pop();
7  }
```

With that the listing below provides a complete parser for an infix expression.

Listing 11.8: Parse Numeric Expression

```
1  int evaluate(const char* expr) {
2    std::stack<operation> ops;
3    std::stack<int> vals;
4    for (expr; expr && *expr; ++expr) {
5      switch (*expr) {
6        case '+':
7          while (!ops.empty()
8                  && ops.top() == times) {
9            apply_top(&ops, &vals);
10         }
11         ops.push(plus);
12         break;
13       case '*':
14         ops.push(times);
15         break;
16       case '(':
17         ops.push(paren);
18         break;
19       case ')':
20         while (ops.top() != paren)
21           apply_top(&ops, &vals);
22         ops.pop();
23         break;
24       default:
25         vals.push(*expr-'0');
26         break;
27     }
28   }
29   while (!ops.empty()) apply_top(&ops, &vals);
30   return vals.top();
31 }
```

The final solution is easily understood as the composition of the two partial solutions. As such, it is easier to reconstruct from remembering the sub problems than it is to reconstruct from itself.

Chapter 12

Subsequences

Subsequences are a generalization of substrings. Substrings are required to be contiguous; they are sub-arrays of sequences. However, subsequences are not required to be contiguous. As such, subsequence search problems are much richer than substring search problems. Subsequences offer a domain of problems including sub structure identification, global structure understanding, and finding relationships between the elements of the sequence.

In this section, we look at problems with solutions that improve on naive enumeration approaches available to sequence and subsequence problems. We begin by examining the standard interview problem of finding a missing value in a sequence. Second, we look at finding elements of a sequence whose sum has required qualities. We then consider problems from machine learning about finding branch points in sequences. Lastly, we look at the questions of finding a substructure with the largest sum in both arrays and matrices.

12.1   Find the missing value

The following is the classic sequential search question. Suppose you are given a vector of size $n - 1$. The vector is unordered, and it is missing exactly one value from the sequence of 1 to n. Find the missing element.

A straightforward solution is to sort the array and scan for the missing element. This solution avoids the difficulty that the elements are not in order. So if they were ordered, the first time we find that an element is not an integral increment of the previous we know the solution.

Listing 12.1: Find the Missing Value by Sorting

```
1   unsigned find_missing_value(
2       std::vector<unsigned> values) {
3     std::sort(values.begin(), values.end());
4     for (auto i = values.begin();
5          i != values.end();
6          ++i) {
7       auto index = i - values.begin() + 1;
8       if (*i != index) {
9         return index;
10      }
11    }
12    return values.size() + 1;
13  }
```

This solution is correct, however the worst case run time of the solution is that of the sort $O(n \log n)$. Worse, we must either manipulate the input or use an extra $O(n)$ amount of space in copying the input.

To do better we must avoid the sort. Since we know the input has structure, we can avoid the sort by scanning the vector and marking every element, we encounter in a lookup table. Such a solution seems straightforward, and in interest of saving space, we would be inclined to use a Boolean array.

```
   Listing 12.2: Find the Missing Value by Tally
1  unsigned find_missing_value(
2      const std::vector<unsigned>& values) {
3      std::vector<bool> bits(values.size()+1, false);
4      for (auto& val : values) bits[val] = true;
5      for (auto i = 1; i < bits.size(); ++i) {
6          if (!bits[i]) return i;
7      }
8      return values.size() + 1;
9  }
```

This solution is clearly linear; we traverse the sequence once and then traverse the Boolean array once. However, it has the distinct disadvantage of requiring memory proportional to n and memory writes. How could we avoid this? One way would require a simple trick learned in algebra long ago, and rediscovered by Gauss when he was in elementary school. The sum of the first n integers is equal to $S_n = n(n-1)/2$. The fact that this holds comes from observing that $1 + n = 2 + (n-1) = 3 + (n-2)$, and $n/2$ such pairs can be collected from the sequence $1, 2, \ldots n$.

So our final solution is to add up the terms in the vector, and subtract that sum from $n(n-1)/2$. Since the sum will be $n(n-1)/2 - k$, where k is the missing value, the missing value will result.

```
   Listing 12.3: Find the Missing Value by Summation
1  unsigned find_missing_value(
2      const std::vector<unsigned>& values) {
3      unsigned n = values.size() + 1;
4      unsigned total = n * (n + 1) / 2;
5      unsigned sum = std::accumulate(values.begin(),
6                                     values.end(),
7                                     0);
8      return total - sum;
9  }
```

Even here there is one issue that we must consider–overflow.

If $n(n-1)$ is greater than the maximum integer representation then this solution will not work because we will not be able to count that high using fixed precision integers. There are many ways of avoiding this complication; but the simplest is using an integer representation for integers that is twice as large than the number of bits as n. We need not much more precision since n^2 can be represented in $2log(n)$ bits. However, if precision becomes a problem due to a high number of elements, sorting may be the only efficient solution.

12.2   Find two members that sum to k

A modification of the previous problem has an interesting solution. Suppose we have a set $\mathbb{S}$ of integers, and we are given a target k. How can we efficiently find two values in the vector that sum to k?

The naive solution is to iterate over all pairs in the list, taking the sum and comparing that to k. This naive solution has quadratic running time since there are $n(n-1)/2$ pairs. To do better will require a bit of thought.

The way to tackle this problem is to convert the problem space from one in which we consider pairs to a search for a single value. Notice that k is not determined by the sequence. So we can consider the sequence $k - \mathbb{S}$ of elements of $\mathbb{S}$ subtracted from k. What is left is a set of targets, and we have a solution if any target is again an element of $\mathbb{S}$. So we have reduced our problem from the search for pairs to the intersection of two sets.

Listing 12.4: Find Values With Sum

```
1  std::tuple<bool, int, int> find_sum_to_k(
2      const std::vector<int>& values,
3      int k) {
4    auto double_trouble = 0;
5    std::set<int> differences;;
6    for (auto& val : values) {
7      auto difference = k - val;
8      if (difference == val) ++double_trouble;
9      differences.insert(difference);
10   }
11   for (auto& val : values) {
12     if (differences.end()!=differences.find(val)){
13       if (val == (k-val) && double_trouble == 1) {
14         continue;
15       }
16       return std::make_tuple(true, val, k - val);
17     }
18   }
19   return std::make_tuple(false, 0, 0);
20 }
```

Note that a sort is at the heart of this solution. The creation of $k - \mathbb{S}$ is linear in the size of the vector, but discovering the intersection can only be done efficiently by sorting $\mathbb{S}$ and $k - \mathbb{S}$. In this case, sorting is not troublesome, since integers are fixed width. We can use a radix sort that completes in linear time.

However, if we resign ourselves to sorting, there is a more straightforward way to answer the question that does not require extra memory.

Suppose that the vector S as sorted in ascending order. Consider the sum $S[0] + S[n - 1]$. If this sum was less than k, then we should increment the left hand index since $S[i] < S[i + 1]$ for all indexes implies $S[0] + S[n - 1] < S[1] + S[n - 1]$. If the sum was greater than k, then we should decrement the right hand index.

This leads to the following solution.

```
1  std::tuple<bool, int, int> find_sum_to_k(
2      std::vector<int> values,
3      int k) {
4      radix_sort(values.begin(), values.end());
5      auto i = values.begin(), j = values.end() - 1;
6      while (i < j) {
7          auto sum = *i + *j;
8          if (k == sum) {
9              return std::make_tuple(true, *i, *j);
10         }
11         if (k < sum) { --j; continue; }
12         ++i;
13     }
14     return std::make_tuple(false, 0, 0);
15  }
```

So we have a simple linear search.

12.3   Find two members with sum closest to zero

Our next demonstration of this technique demonstrates its power. Consider the same set up, but now the problem is finding the two elements of a sequence whose sum is closest to zero.

Using the absolute value function, we can apply the same technique to find a solution. The only modification is that we must track the smallest found value.

Listing 12.6: Find Values With Sum Closest to 0

```cpp
std::tuple<int, int, int> find_sum_closest_to_0(
    std::vector<int>& values) {
  if (values.size() < 2) throw std::exception();
  radix_sort(values.begin(), values.end());
  std::tuple<int, int, int> a_b_sum(
      0, 0, std::numeric_limits<int>::max());
  auto a = values.begin(), b = values.end() - 1;
  while (a < b) {
    auto sum = *a + *b;
    auto abs = std::abs(sum);
    if (abs < std::get<2>(a_b_sum)) {
      a_b_sum = std::make_tuple(*a, *b, abs);
    }
    if (sum < 0) ++a;
    else --b;
  }
  return a_b_sum;
}
```

A fixed target simplifies this problem, and we next we generalize this to finding to elements that are closest to a moving target.

12.4 Find two members that sum to a third

The technique of using a radix-sort and linear scan discussed above has many applications. Consider the problem of deciding if finding a triple x, y, and z such that $x + y = z$ from a vector S of n integers.

A simple quadratic algorithm is available. We use radix sort again to sort the set of integers in linear time. Then, for each element c of the vector call the previous procedure with $k = c$. We construct the search sequence from the sorted sequence. This avoids repeated sorting.

Listing 12.7: Find Values With Sum to A Third

```
1  std::tuple<bool, int, int, int> find_sum_to_c(
2      std::vector<int>& values) {
3      radix_sort(values.begin(), values.end());
4      for (auto& c : values) {
5          auto a = values.begin(), b = values.end() - 1;
6          while (a < b) {
7              if (&c == &*a) { ++a; continue; }
8              if (&c == &*b) { --b; continue; }
9              auto sum = *a + *b - c;
10             if (0 == sum) {
11                 return std::make_tuple(true, *a, *b, c);
12             } else if (sum > 0) --b;
13             else ++a;
14         }
15     }
16     return std::make_tuple(false, 0, 0, 0);
17 }
```

It is always satisfying to see previous solutions finding new uses.

12.5   Find the maximum difference

Let's continue with a vector S of n integers but examine different techniques. Now consider finding a pair i, j of indices with $i < j$ that maximize the difference $s[j] - s[i]$. What makes this an interesting question is the requirement of order, that $i < j$. Without it we simply need to find the minimum and maximum elements of S that can be done in a linear scan.

As usual, this problem has a naive quadratic solution that involves considering every pairs i, j with $j > i$ and tracking the maximum. What makes this naive is that it is a brute force solution that does not consider the input domain or the structure of the problem.

To see the solution, consider what pairs we should consider for the index j. Let's suppose that j is the right hand index, so we need only look at elements of S that precede j. The difference $s[j] - s[i]$ is maximized for the index i that contains the minimum element of $s[1], ... s[j - 1]$.

Listing 12.8: Find Max Difference

```cpp
int find_max_difference(
    const std::vector<int> values) {
    if (values.size() < 2) throw std::exception();
    int max = std::numeric_limits<int>::min();
    auto min = values.begin();
    auto i = values.begin() + 1;
    while (i != values.end()) {
      max = std::max(max, *i - *min);
      if (*i < *min) min = i;
      ++i;
    }
    return max;
}
```

Therefore, instead of looking over pairs, we need only keep track of the minimum element preceding any other index. As shown above, that can be done with a linear scan.

12.6   Pivot maximizing difference

Suppose now you have a sequence of elements that are only either 0 or 1. Find the index i that maximizes the difference in structure of the sequence. That is, find i to maximize that the sum of the number of 0s (or 1s) in the set $\{s[0], ...s[i-1]\}$ and the number of 1's (or 0's) in the set $s[i], ...s[n-1]$.

The solution to this question is to make two passes. The first pass calculates the number of 1's in the sequence. The second pass then finds the pivot point by scanning from beginning to end, and tracking the number of 1's encountered. In the second pass, at each index we know the prefix size and the count of 1's encountered. The number of zeros in the prefix is the length of the prefix minus the partial count. The number of ones in the suffix is the total count minus the partial count.

Lets denote by $lhs(i)$ the number of elements of value i in the prefix, and by $rhs(i)$ the number of elements of value i in the suffix. Then since each element is either 0 or 1, we have

$$lhs(0) + rhs(1) + rhs(0) + lhs(1) = |S|$$

That is from the prefix values, we know the values in the opposite direction.

Listing 12.9: Find Max Difference

```
1  std::vector<bool>::const_iterator partition_index(
2      const std::vector<bool>& v) {
3    auto total_sum = std::accumulate(
4      v.begin(), v.end(), 0);
5    auto best_sum = std::max<int>(
6      total_sum, v.size() - total_sum);
7    auto partition = v.end();
8    auto current_sum = 0;
9    for (auto i = v.begin(); i != v.end(); ++i) {
10     if (*i) ++current_sum;
11     auto left_zeros = 1+(i-v.begin())-current_sum;
12     auto right_ones = total_sum - current_sum;
13     auto sum = std::max<int>(
14       left_zeros + right_ones,
15       v.size() - left_zeros - right_ones);
16     if (sum >= best_sum) {
17       best_sum = sum;
18       partition = i;
19     }
20   }
21   return partition;
22 }
```

This problem has uses in machine learning for finding the best branch point from a sequence of observations.

12.7　Pivot closest to equal sums

Consider next the problem of finding a pivot element in a vector of integers such that the difference between the each side is minimized. That is to find the pivot point that minimizes the difference in the sum of the elements of each side.

The problem is only interesting in so much as we can do better than the naive quadratic solution. It is also an application of the same technique above, where once we know the sum of the entire vector; we can keep a running total to calculate the sum of any subset and its complement.

Listing 12.10: Find Pivot Minimizing Difference

```cpp
std::vector<int>::const_iterator partition_index(
    const std::vector<int>& v) {
  auto total_sum = std::accumulate(
    v.begin(), v.end(), 0);
  auto sum = 0;
  auto index = v.end();
  auto lowest = std::abs(total_sum);
  for (auto val = v.begin(); val!=v.end(); ++val) {
    sum += *val;
    auto difference = std::abs(total_sum - 2*sum);
    if (difference <= lowest) {
      lowest = difference;
      index = val;
    }
  }
  return index;
}
```

That final linear algorithm completes our look at numerical sequences and partitioning. We next consider finding maximum substructures.

12.8 Maximum sub-array

In my experience, the following problem is the most common sequence question asked. Given a vector of integers S, find the maximum of the sum of any sub-array. That is any in which all the elements are adjacent in S.

Note that the only non trivial question that could be asked is in finding contiguous subsequences. The subsequence with the largest sum is clearly one of two choices; all non-negative values or that of the largest single negative value.

The naive solution is costly. The first is that the naive solution is cubic. To see this note that we require $n(n-1)/2$ pairs of indexes to exhaust the indexes of all subsequences. To find the sum of any subsequence we need to add every element in each of the sub-arrays.

To do better, consider an update rule for sub-arrays. Suppose that the sum of a sub-array is negative. Then, unless this sub-array achieves the maximum, it cannot be the beginning or end of any subsequence achieving the maximum. So once such a sub-array has been identified it can be discarded, since removing it from any other sub-array will only increase the sum of the elements.

Listing 12.11: Maximum Sub-Array

```
1  int max_subarray(const std::vector<int>& v) {
2    if (v.empty()) return 0;
3    auto sum = 0;
4    auto max = std::numeric_limits<int>::min();
5    for (auto& val : v) {
6      sum += val;
7      max = std::max(max, sum);
8      sum = std::max(sum, 0);
9    }
10   return max;
11 }
```

Clearly, this algorithm is linear. That is a drastic improvement from the cubic naive solution.

12.9   Maximum sub-matrix

We conclude with a problem that generalizes the from sequences to arrays. The maximum sub-matrix problem asks to identify the sub-matrix whose sum of elements is largest.

To state the problem precisely, suppose we are given a matrix M with dimensions m and n. We wish to identify the sub-matrix M' bounded by indexes (i, j) and (s, t) such that $\sum_{M'}$ is the largest.

The naive solution simply enumerates all possible coordinates bounding a sub-matrix and calculates the sum of each. As there are $O(m^2 n^2)$ pairs, summing all of the entries in each sub-matrix is a task with run time $O(m^3 n^3)$.

As in the maximum sub-array problem, we want to identify a

means of avoiding summing each sub-matrix. A standard trick is to use dynamic programming to pre-compute the sum of each sub-matrix with top-left coordinate at $(0,0)$. This creates a lookup table. Given this lookup table, we can compute the sum of the matrix bounded by (i,j) and (s,t) as $m[s,t]+m[i,j]-m[i,t]-m[s,j]$. The second summand double counts the top left corner sub-matrix, and the last two remove from the sum the top rows and left columns.

In the listing below, we enumerate all coordinates, and calculate the sum of each sub-matrix using the lookup table defined previously. Observe that we are careful to enumerate the sub-matrixes extending to the boundaries of the matrix as well as the sub-matrix bounded by both coordinates.

Listing 12.12: Maximum Sub-Matrix

```
1  int max_submatrix(matrix m) {
2    auto max = std::numeric_limits<int>::min();
3    for (auto row = 0; row < m.size(); ++row) {
4      for (auto col = 0; col < m[0].size(); ++col) {
5        m[row][col] = m[row][col]
6          + (row > 0 ? m[row-1][col] : 0)
7          + (col > 0 ? m[row][col-1] : 0)
8          - (row > 0 && col > 0 ?
9              m[row-1][col-1] : 0);
10       }
11     }
12   for (auto trow = 0; trow < m.size(); ++trow) {
13   for (auto tcol = 0; tcol < m[0].size(); ++tcol){
14   for (auto brow = trow; brow < m.size(); ++brow){
15   for (auto bcol =tcol; bcol <m[0].size();++bcol){
16     auto top = m[trow][tcol];
17     auto left =  m[brow][tcol];
18     auto up =  m[trow][bcol];
19     auto bottom = m[brow][bcol];
20     max = std::max(max, bottom + top - up - left);
21     max = std::max(max, bottom - up);
22     max = std::max(max, bottom - left);
23     max = std::max(max, bottom);
24   }}}}
25   return max;
26 }
```

As we now avoid the unnecessary sums, we have a quartic solution.

To do better requires a clever trick. As this problem is a generalization of the maximum sub-array problem, it is not a surprise that we can use the algorithm developed previously as a sub-procedure in an optimal solution.

The goal is to find a means to avoid enumerating all quartic pairs of sub-matrix bounds. To see how this is done, first consider what results from constructing a matrix M' by summing row-wise. That is replacing $m[i][j]$ with $m'[i][j] = \sum_{k \leq j} m[i][j]$. The result is similar to the lookup table above. Given any two entries in a row M'_i, we easily calculate the sum of the elements in the sub-array of the row M_i bounded by those entries by taking the difference. Observe that the column of values $M'^j - M'^t$ is the sum of the elements in the row bounded by column j and t. And the sum of the elements in this column from i to j is exactly the sum of the elements in the sub-matrix of M bounded by indexes (i, j) and (s, t).

So taking all pairs of columns of M', we can enumerate every sub-matrix. And for each pair of columns, the solution to the maximum sub-array problem allows us to find the sub-matrix in that cone in linear time by scanning column-wise.

```
     Listing 12.13: Maximum Sub-Matrix in Cubic Time
 1   int max_submatrix(matrix m) {
 2     auto max = std::numeric_limits<int>::min();
 3     for (auto& row : m) {
 4       int sum = 0;
 5       for (auto& val : row) {
 6         sum += val;
 7         val = sum;
 8       }
 9     }
10     for (auto col = 0;
11          !m.empty() && col < m[0].size();
12          ++col) {
13     for (auto col2 = col;
14          col2 < m[0].size();
15          ++col2) {
16       std::vector<int> diff(m.size());
17       for (auto row = 0; row < m.size(); ++row) {
18         diff[row] = m[row][col2];
19         if (col2 != col) {
20           diff[row] -= m[row][col];
21         }
22         max = std::max(max, max_subarray(diff));
23       }
24     }}
25     return max;
26   }
```

We've reduced the asymptotic run time to $O(mn^2)$. And not only is satisfying to be able to re-use work that we've produced before, this solution is refreshing in its simplicity.

Chapter 13

Recursion

In its simplest form, recursion occurs when a function is references itself. By doing so, it is using the execution stack as temporary storage to compute solutions to subproblems without interrupting the current state of the program.

Recursion is a programming technique that takes practice to use and understand. When reading code, the problem with recursion is that on first pass a recursive solution does not seem to solve a problem in its entirety. The problem with writing a recursive solution is that on first pass a recursive solution does not seen strong enough to solve a problem in its entirely. However, first impressions are often misleading.

The first step to using recursion is finding the smallest functional step that makes progress towards a solution in a smaller problem. Afterward it is usually a matter of only iterating that step as many times as necessary until the problem is solved. Recursion is also called the *divide and conquer* method. To use recursion efficiently subproblems should be simpler or smaller. Recursive branch points should reduce the problem size by a constant fraction. Otherwise, while recursion will get us closer to the solution, it may do so at the cost of high memory usage. Since the stack is bounded, high memory usage of recursion leads stack overflow errors.

In this chapter, we will look at the commonly asked problems that are best solved with recursion. First, we consider calculating the summation and factorial of values. Second, we discuss and solve the famous Towers of Hanoi problem. We conclude with the N-Queens problem.

13.1   Factorial and summation

In the study of algorithms, the first exposure of recursion is its use in
computing a summation and factorial. In programming interviews,
a warm up questions of factorial or summation can be used to direct
the candidates thinking along the lines of using recursion.

In summation, the question is to compute the sum of the natural
numbers up to n. The recursive solution is that this sum is equal to
n plus the sum of the natural numbers up to $n - 1$. In this solution,
we are reducing the problem by a single step and then recursing.
In code, this may look like the following.

Listing 13.1: Recursive Summation

```
1  unsigned int sum_to_n(unsigned int n) {
2    if (n == 0) return 0;
3    return n + sum_to_n(n-1);
4  }
```

Factorial is the product of the first n natural numbers. A listing
for factorial can be written similarly.

Listing 13.2: Recursive Factorial

```
1  unsigned int factorial(unsigned int n) {
2    if (n == 1) return 1;
3    return n * factorial(n-1);
4  }
```

In both of these listings, the return value of the recursive call is
modified before it is returned to the previous caller in the recursive
chain. This inefficiency can sometimes by optimized by *tail recursion*.
A tail call is one in which the computed value is returned directly
to the parent without modification. Tail recursion simplifies the
recursive structure of the solution such that the final solution is
returned directly to the caller bypassing the entirely of the recursive
call stack. Hence for instance, a tail recursive summation could be
written as.

Listing 13.3: Tail-Recursive Summation

```
1  unsigned int sum_to_n(unsigned int n,
2                        unsigned int total = 0) {
3    if (n == 0) return total;
4    return sum_to_n(n-1, total + n);
5  }
```

Notice that the declaration of the method is different. Above we need to send two parameters in the function call, and we do a small unit of work prior to the recursive call. This is a hallmark of tail recursion.

For completeness, the tail recursive form of the factorial function is below.

Listing 13.4: Tail-Recursive Factorial

```
1  unsigned int factorial(unsigned int n,
2                         unsigned int prod = 1) {
3    if (n == 1) return prod;
4    return factorial(n-1, prod * n);
5  }
```

Note that as above the majority of the calculation is done prior to the tail call.

13.2 Towers of Hanoi

The most common interview question with a simple recursive solution is the *Towers of Hanoi*. In this problem, we consider three pegs. On the first peg are n disks of increasing size, from smallest on top to the largest on the bottom. n can be any number, the question is generally posed with $n = 3$. The problem is to move all the disks from the first peg to the last peg, obeying two rules. First, only moving one disk may be moved at a time and always to the top of the stack on a peg. Second, a larger disk may never be moved on top of a smaller disk.

To develop a recursive solution, we start by considering the first rule. To that end, suppose we have a function that moves the top most disk from peg i to peg j. We will declare this function as:

```
1  void move(int from, int to);
```

Now, how would we solve the problem using this method? Let us simplify and consider the problem with a single disk, or $n = 1$. We move the first peg to the third, and the problem is solved. Suppose then there are two disks, or $n = 2$. We have to move the top disk to a temporary peg, complete the single disk problem, and finally move the second disk to its final location. Immediately we see that there is some recursive structure as the $n = 2$ problem used the $n = 1$ problem as a solution.

Can we use the $n = 2$ case to solve the problem with three disks? Indeed, we can. However, to do so requires the mental leap from a simple iterative solution to the recursive one. The leap is to see that we are not looking to take a single step and then recurse. Instead it is to solve the $n - 1$ case for a temporary peg, solve the $n = 1$ case, and then recurse with a relabeling of the pegs. So in the 3−disk problem, we first solve the 2−disk problem for a temporary peg, solve the problem for the remaining single disk, and then recurse on the reduced problem of the remaining two disks with the third already in place. We can see this in code in the following listing.

```
     Listing 13.6: Towers of Hanoi Solution
 1   void hanoi(int num, int src, int dest, int temp)
 2   {
 3       if (num == 1) {
 4           move(src, temp);
 5           return;
 6       }
 7       hanoi(num-1, src, temp, dest);
 8       hanoi(1, src, dest, temp);
 9       hanoi(num-1, temp, dest, src);
10   }
```

Studying this solution note the following. The first recursion call solves recursive problem of moving $n-1$ disks to the temporary peg. We then move the largest peg to its final spot. Finally, a last recursive call is made to move the remaining disks from the temporary peg to the destination. Note that the each step only affects a relabeling of source, destination, and temporary storage.

13.3 N-Queens problem

Often, complex graph problems have simple recursive solutions. The reason is that we can make a move, say visit a node or eliminate a number of possibilities, and recurse then on the problem in a new state. Such is the final problem in this section, the *N-Queens Problem*.

In this problem, we have an $n \times n$ chessboard, and we wish to find all placements of n queens such that no two queens could capture each other. Concretely, the 8 Queens problem involves placing 8 queens on the standard 8×8 chess board such that no two queens share any row, column, or diagonal. As n increases, so do the number of solutions. In fact, for the 8 Queens problems there are 96 solutions but only 12 unique up to rotations.

Let us start by describing the problem in more detail. The chessboard can be represented by a sequence of pairs identifying each square. So for example, the coordinate x, y represents the square at row x and column y. We agree to label the top left square as $0, 0$. So a single solution to the 8−Queens problems is a set of

8 pairs of coordinates each representing the placement of a queen within that solution. The following type definitions formalize this.

Listing 13.7: *N*-Queens Types

```
1  typedef std::tuple<int, int> Square;
2  typedef std::set<Square> Solution;
3  typedef std::set<Solution> SolutionSet;
```

Let us begin by considering simple cases in hopes of finding a recursive solution. For the 1−Queen problem, there is but a single solution. We place a queen, and in doing so eliminate a row and column. This exhausts the search space, and we have found a solution. Now for $n = 2$ and $n = 3$ the problem does not have a simple recursive solution. The reason is that there is no solution at all. For any position a queen can be placed in the 2−Queen problem, that queen can move to any other square on the board making placing a second queen impossible. Further, for any position a queen can be placed in the 3−Queen problem, the reduced problem is the impossible to solve 2−Queen problem.

Skip ahead to the 4−Queens problem. Let's start by enumerating where the first queen could be placed. Suppose then we place the first queen in the top corner at coordinates 0, 0. Such a placement would reduce the search space for the following 3 queens by eliminating the first row, the first column, and the diagonal starting at the top left corner of the board and extending down to the bottom right. After this move there are only 6 possible coordinates for the second queen. And each coordinate is a combination of one of the remaining 3 rows and 3 columns. Note that while every solution exhausts all the rows and columns, not every diagonal is covered by a queen. So we do not have a need to enumerate diagonals, only ensure that we do not cover one twice. So now, if we place the second queen at coordinate 3, 1, then we need to mark the upward leaning diagonal from 3, 1 to 1, 3 as unavailable. We address the downward-diagonals and upward-diagonals by the coordinate of the first row and column they encounter on the board coming from their perspective directions. Hence the downward diagonal for coordinate $(0, 0)$ is $(0, 0)$. The downward diagonal crossing $(1, 1)$ is again $(0, 0)$. Similarly, with our definition upward diagonal crossing $(2, 3)$ and

$(3,2)$ is denoted $(3,2)$. The following utility functions make this precise.

Listing 13.8: *N*-Queens Diagonal Identification

```
1  Square normalize_downward(int row, int col) {
2    while (row && col) { --row; --col; }
3    return std::make_tuple(row, col);
4  }
5  Square normalize_upward(int row, int col, int dim){
6    while (row && col < (dim -1)) { --row; ++col; }
7    return std::make_tuple(row, col);
8  }
```

Note that we start with n rows and n columns. Further, we can choose from n downward sloping diagonals and n upward sloping diagonals. In a solution to the *N*-Queens problem, every row, column, downward-diagonal, and upward-diagonal must be covered. To do so, we can continue iterating through the available rows, columns, downward-diagonals, and upward-diagonals until we have exhausted them all. To track the state of our search we use the structure defined in the following listing.

Listing 13.9: *N*-Queens State Information

```
1  struct NQueensState {
2    int dim;
3    std::set<int> rows;
4    std::set<int> cols;
5    std::set<Square> down_diag;
6    std::set<Square> up_diag;
7    explicit NQueensState(int n) : dim(n) {
8      for (auto i = 0; i < n; ++i) rows.insert(i);
9      for (auto i = 0; i < n; ++i) cols.insert(i);
10   }
11 };
```

Putting this together we have our following listing for finding a solution to the *N*-Queens problem using recursion.

Listing 13.10: *N*-Queens Solution

```
1  void nqueens(
2      NQueensState* state,
3      SolutionSet* solutions,
4      Solution board = Solution()) {
5    if (state->rows.empty() &&
6        state->cols.empty()) {
7      if (!board.empty()) solutions->insert(board);
8      return;
9    }
10   for (auto row: state->rows) {
11     for (auto col: state->cols) {
12       Square downward_coord = normalize_downward(
13           row, col);
14       Square upward_coord = normalize_upward(
15           row, col, state->dim);
16       if (state->down_diag.end() !=
17               state->down_diag.find(downward_coord)
18           || state->up_diag.end() !=
19               state->up_diag.find(upward_coord)) {
20         continue;
21       }
22       NQueensState new_state = *state;
23       new_state.rows.erase(row);
24       new_state.cols.erase(col);
25       new_state.down_diag.insert(downward_coord);
26       new_state.up_diag.insert(upward_coord);
27       Solution new_board(board);
28       new_board.insert(std::make_tuple(row, col));
29       nqueens(&new_state, solutions, new_board);
30     }
31   }
32 }
```

The solution above attempts to blindly enumerate all possible positions of n queens on an $n \times n$ chessboard. The only heuristics is pruning invalid states before placement of the next queen, a queen is not placed if it would capture another. As such, the solution has an exponential run time.

Engineers often view recursion as inefficient and dangerous, and don't be surprised to hear the follow up to a recursive solution

"Now do it iteratively." In the case of factorial, where an iterative solution can avoid both pushing on the stack and the function call this is a worthwhile follow up. Some graphical problems such as recursive depth first search can also be simplified by using an explicit stack instead of the implicit execution stacks. With recursion, stack overflow is to be checked.

However, recursion provides succinctness to a solution that cannot be found with complex iterative solutions. In addition, the insight that can be gained from a recursive solution, either in the construction of a solution or the search of a problem space, is often lost in the index and memory management ubiquitous to iterative solutions.

Tail recursive solutions are as computationally efficient as iterative solutions when the recursive depth is not extra-ordinary. In addition, the main benefit of using recursion is the simplicity of the solution. A recursive solution for both the Towers of Hanoi and the N-Queens Problem has fewer special cases and fewer lines of code than iterative solutions

If a recursive problem presents itself, you should never by shy to provide it. But be prepared to justify its use by judging the depth of recursion.

Chapter 14

Dynamic Programming

Dynamic programming refers to a method of solving problems using a bottom up approach. Starting with a simple base case, iteratively larger sub problems are solved in sequence. These simpler problems are designed to increase in complexity and culminate in the final solution.

Application of dynamic programming follows three steps. The first one develops the proper relation as an update rule. This relation usually takes the form of an equation solving for the $n^t h$ case in terms of previously solved cases indexed by 0 to $n - 1$. The second step translates the update rule into an efficient implementation. This is usually straightforward. The last step is to backtrack from the set of solutions produced to reconstruct the solution. Backtracking involves unwinding the computational tree that we evaluated.

Theoretically, dynamic programming can address optimization problems if they have optimal substructure and overlapping sub problems. Optimal substructure refers to the property that an optimal solution can be found by efficiently modifying the optimal solution of smaller problems. Overlapping sub problems refers to the property that a solution can be written as a tree of sub problems in an inductive manner. Often these two properties are obvious from the discovery of an update rule.

Dynamic programming is a powerful technique that reveals hidden substructure and uncovers insight into a problem. This insight often leads to optimal solutions that require work beyond a mechanical application of dynamic programming. In this section, we endeavor to make clear the techniques in application of dynamic programming at the cost of optimality in running time or space.

In this section, we will apply dynamic programming to a number of programming problems. First, we study that classic problem of the longest common subsequence. We then look at determining the longest increasing subsequence. Next, we compute the edit distance between two strings. Lastly, we discover a pseudo-polynomial solution to the problem of creating equal partitions.

14.1 Longest common subsequence

The most common application of dynamic programming is finding the longest common subsequence of two sequences. This is a much different question from the longest common sub-array, in that the entries of a subsequence need not be adjacent.

Dynamic programming can be used to solve this problem because it has optimal substructure and overlapping sub problems. To see this let us develop an update rule.

Suppose we have two sequences S and T of length m and n. Let us denote by (S, T) the longest common subsequence. Now if either are empty, then clearly $(S, T) = \emptyset$. Suppose then that neither is empty.

Denote by S_i the prefix of S of length i and by T_j be prefix of T of length j. We can calculate $(S, T) = (S_m, T_n)$ from the sub problems (S_{m-1}, T_{n-1}), (S_{m-1}, T_n) and (S_m, T_{n-1}). For if $s[m] = t[n]$, then the longest common subsequence of (S_{m-1}, T_{n-1}) is extended by one. However if the last two values disagree, then we do not extend the longest common subsequence of either of the adjacent sequences (S_{m-1}, T_n) or (S_m, T_{n-1}). Note that we need to know both adjacent subsequences. (S_{m-1}, T_{n-1}) may be used to get us from the longest common subsequence by extending either S_{m-1} or T_{n-1}. We have developed the following update rule.

$$(S_i, T_j) = \begin{cases} \emptyset, \text{ if } S_i = \emptyset \text{ or } T_j = \emptyset. \text{ Otherwise} \\ \max \begin{cases} 1 + (S_{i-1}, T_{j-1}) & \text{if s[i]} = \text{t[j]}, \\ (S_{i-1}, T_j) \\ (S_i, T_{j-1}) \end{cases} \end{cases}$$

That the maximum (S, T) depends on the maximum of the sub problems shows the property of optimal sub problems. That every intermediate problem recurses back to the base case of an empty sequence is the property of overlapping sub problems. And these are the requirements for dynamic programming to provably result in an optimal solution.

From the update rule, we see that the problem can be solved by starting with the empty prefixes, namely $(S_0, T_j) = 0$ for all j and $(S_i, T_0) = 0$ for all i. We increase the length of S by one, and then compute the sub problems for $T_1, T_2, \ldots T_n$ in that order. We continue in this fashion until the problem is solved with the calculation of (S, T).

To implement the algorithm we will want to memoize the values of the sub problems in a matrix indexed by the length of the prefixes considered. There are two options. For each sub problem, we can store the optimal subsequence. Alternatively, for each sub problem we can store the length of the subsequence. As we shall see, storing the length alone will allow us to reconstruct the longest common subsequence with only a little patience.

Listing 14.1: Longest Common Subsequence With Backtracking

```
 1  std::vector<int> longest_common_subsequence(
 2      const std::vector<int>& s,
 3      const std::vector<int>& t) {
 4      std::vector<std::vector<int>> memo(
 5          s.size() + 1,
 6          std::vector<int>(t.size() + 1, 0));
 7      for (auto i = 0; i < s.size() + 1; ++i) {
 8          for (auto j = 0; j < t.size() + 1; ++j) {
 9              if (i == 0) memo[i][j] = 0;
10              else if (j == 0) memo[i][j] = 0;
11              else memo[i][j] = (s[i-1] == t[j-1]) ?
12                  1 + memo[i-1][j-1] :
13                  std::max(memo[i-1][j], memo[i][j-1]);
14          }
15      }
16      std::vector<int> lcs;
17      auto length = memo[s.size()][t.size()];
18      for (auto i = s.size(), j = t.size();
19              i && j && length;
20              --length) {
21          while (i && memo[i-1][j] == length) --i;
22          while (j && memo[i][j-1] == length) --j;
23          lcs.emplace(lcs.begin(), s[i-1]);
24      }
25      return lcs;
26  }
```

The second half of the listing above extracts the subsequence from the memoized matrix constructed by dynamic programming. This process is called backtracking and is common in dynamic programming.

The previous solution has two nested loops and constructs the full $m \times n$ matrix of partial solutions. As such, it requires both quadratic time and space.

Consider for a moment what changes could be made if the problem was only to return the length of the longest subsequence. We need not backtrack in this case, we do not require the full transition matrix to be available at any iteration. Inspection reveals only the three cells are needed; immediately above, behind, and the preceding diagonal. From this we can see that we can save space by memoizing only a single row of calculations if we proceed from left to right. As we would over write the back diagonal of the next iteration, we save this as a temporary during the calculation of one row. Implementing this idea we have a space efficient implementation that removes the need for backtracking.

Listing 14.2: Longest Common Subsequence

```
int longest_common_subsequence(
    const std::vector<int>& s,
    const std::vector<int>& t) {
  std::vector<int> memo(t.size() + 1, 0);
  for (auto i = 1; i < s.size() + 1; ++i) {
    auto previous_diagonol =
      memo.size() ? memo[0] : 0;
    for (auto j = 1; j < t.size() + 1; ++j) {
      auto temp = memo[j];
      memo[j] = (s[i-1] == t[j-1]) ?
        1 + previous_diagonol :
        std::max(memo[j], memo[j-1]);
      previous_diagonol = temp;
    }
  }
  return memo[t.size()];
}
```

This final implementation has running time of $O(n * m)$, and requires only linear space. It is an efficient implementation of dynamic programming.

14.2 Longest increasing subsequence

A companion problem to the longest common subsequence is that of finding the longest increasing subsequence of a sequence. That is a subsequence T of S for which $t[i] \leq t[j]$ whenever $i \leq j$.

As before denote by S_i the prefix of S of length i, and now let (S_i) be the length of the longest increasing subsequence of S_i ending with $s[i]$. Note that $s[i]$ is a possible increase of all other subsequences before it. From this observation, we can see the update rule for longest increasing subsequence.

$$(S_i) = \begin{cases} 0, \text{ if } i = 0 \\ 1 + \max\{(S_j) : j < i, s[j] < s[i]\} \end{cases}$$

Implementing this update rule is straightforward.

Listing 14.3: Longest Increasing Subsequence

```cpp
int longest_increasing_subsequence(
    const std::vector<int>& s) {
  if (s.empty()) return 0;
  std::vector<int> memo(s.size(), 1);
  for (auto i = 0; i < s.size(); ++i) {
    for (auto j = 0; j < i; ++j) {
      if (s[i] >= s[j]) {
        memo[i] = std::max(1 + memo[j], memo[i]);
      }
    }
  }
  return *std::max_element(memo.begin(),
                           memo.end());
}
```

As is easily seen, the solution above has quadratic running time due to the nested loop.

The problem can be approach another way. A second solution reveals a relationship between the longest increasing subsequence and the longest common sequence. We solve the former with a clever application of the longest increasing subsequence algorithm. Consider if we copy S and sort the elements of the sequence, producing T. Then note that a subsequence of S is increasing if and only if it is a common subsequence of T. This bijection is enough to lead directly to the solution.

Listing 14.4: Longest Increasing Subsequence From Longest Common Subsequence

```
1  int longest_increasing_subsequence(
2      const std::vector<int> s) {
3      std::vector<int> t(s.begin(), s.end());
4      std::sort(t.begin(), t.end());
5      return longest_common_subsequence(s, t);
6  }
```

This solution has the same asymptotic running time as above. But while the previous solution avoids the sort, this one provides more satisfaction in that we can re-use what we have developed previously.

14.3 Edit distance

Our next application of dynamic programming will be the classic problem of finding the edit distance between two strings. Edit distance has many uses in computer science and informatics. The edit distance gives a measure of the similarity between two strings, and hence can be used to detect spelling errors string similarity.

The edit distance between two strings is the minimum number of character operations that need be applied to one string to result in the other. There are many types of edit operations. The most common are insertion, deletion, substitution, and transposition.

For example, to convert from the string 'cat' to 'attack' requires a deletion of the letter 'c', and insertion of the suffix 'tack' for a total of 5 operations. There are many other sequences of operations that can be applied, but none have a fewer number of operations.

Each string edit operation can be given a different weight in the calculation of distance, resulting in a different measure of similarity. However, all of them can be solved by applying dynamic programming.

In the following, we consider the problem of calculating two kinds of edit distance that have homogenous weights for their allowed operations; Levenshtein distance and its generalization Damerau-Levenshtein distance.

14.3.1   Levenshtein distance

Levenshtein distance refers to edit distance in which the only single character operations are allowed. These operations are insertion, deletion, and substitution. Each of them imposes a cost of one, which discounts substitution, as it is not considered the same as combination of a delete and insert.

Applying the dynamic programming approach requires us to develop an update rule. Consider the Levenshtein distance between a string and an empty string. Clearly, these will require deletion or insertion of each character respectively. Therefore, the Levenshtein distance must be the length of the non-empty parameter.

As before suppose S_i refers to the first i characters of S. Consider which single transitions can result in (S_i, T_j), the distance between the prefixes of S and T of length i and j respectively. The transitions can be used to calculate the edit distance (S_i, T_j). If $i = 0$ or $j = 0$, we are in the empty substring case above. Suppose then not. We consider each possible operation.

If we transition from S_i to T_j by deleting a character from S_i, then the number of operations is $(S_{i-1}, T_j) + 1$. If we added a character to a substring of T_j then the number of operations is $(S_i, T_{j-1}) + 1$. If we transition along the diagonal then $(S_{i-1}, T_{j-1}) + 1\{s_i \neq t_j\}$. Every transition results in the same state, so we want the minimum value taken over these transitions. This gives us the value of i and j in the transition matrix as

$$
(S_i, T_j) = \begin{cases} i & \text{if } j = 0 \\ j & \text{if } i = 0, \text{ else} \\ \min \begin{cases} (S_{i-1}, T_j) + 1 & \text{(deletion)} \\ (S_i, T_{j-1}) + 1 & \text{(insertion)} \\ (S_{i-1}, T_{j-1}) + 1 & \text{if } s[i] \neq t[j] \text{ (substitution)} \\ (S_{i-1}, T_{j-1}) & \text{if } s[i] = t[j] \end{cases} \end{cases}
$$

From this update rule it is clear that we need to calculate the full matrix to find the Levenshtein of two strings S and T. This is completed in the listing below.

```
     Listing 14.5: Levenshtein Distance
1  int edit_distance(const std::string& s,
2                     const std::string& t) {
3    auto memo =
4      std::vector<std::vector<int>>(
5        s.size() + 1,
6        std::vector<int>(t.size() + 1, 0));
7    for (auto i = 0; i < s.size() + 1; ++i) {
8      for (auto j = 0; j < t.size() + 1; ++j) {
9        if (i == 0) memo[i][j] = j;
10       else if (j == 0) memo[i][j] = i;
11       else {
12         auto deletion = 1 + memo[i-1][j];
13         auto insertion = 1 + memo[i][j-1];
14         auto substitution =
15           memo[i-1][j-1] +
16           ((s[i-1] == t[j-1]) ? 0 : 1);
17         memo[i][j] =
18           std::min(deletion,
19                    std::min(insertion,
20                             substitution));
21       }
22     }
23   }
24   return memo[s.size()][t.size()];
25 }
```

In as much as the only value returned is the Levenshtein distance, the above algorithm is not space optimal. However we memo the entire transition-cost matrix in order to provide a means to backtrack the sequence of edit operations needed to convert S to T.

14.3.2 Damerau-Levenshtein distance

In an effort to identify human misspellings, Damerau identified four edit operations insertion, deletion, substitution, and transposition. A transposition occurs when adjacent letters in a string are swapped. For instance the postal codes "MN" and "NM" differ by only a transposition, but their Levenshtein distance is two.

The Damerau-Levenshtein distance is the minimum number of

the four edit operations needed to transform one string to another. It has uses in identifying human misspellings as well as in identifying mutations in genetics.

To solve the problem of calculating the Damerau-Levenshtein distance we need only modify the update rule from Levenshtein distance above. We transition to a state from a transposition if the new state has at least two characters and the characters have been transposed from the previous state. Formally, we add a single state to the min clause of the update rule for Levenshtein distance.

$$
(S_i, T_j) = \begin{cases} i & \text{if } j = 0 \\ j & \text{if } i = 0, \text{ else} \\ \min \begin{cases} (S_{i-1}, T_j) + 1 & \text{(deletion)} \\ (S_i, T_{j-1}) + 1 & \text{(insertion)} \\ (S_{i-1}, T_{j-1}) + 1 & \text{if } s[i] \neq t[j] \text{ (substitution)} \\ (S_{i-2}, T_{j-2}) + 1 & \begin{array}{l} \text{if } s[i] = t[j-1] \\ \text{and } s[i-1] = t[j] \\ \text{(transposition)} \end{array} \\ (S_{i-1}, T_{j-1}) & \text{if } s[i] = t[j] \end{cases} \end{cases}
$$

A straightforward modification of the previous code translates this extra rule into a listing.

Listing 14.6: Damerau-Levenshtein Distance

```
1  int edit_distance(const std::string& s,
2                     const std::string& t) {
3    auto memo =
4      std::vector<std::vector<int>>(
5        s.size() + 1,
6        std::vector<int>(t.size() + 1, 0));
7    for (auto i = 0; i < s.size() + 1; ++i) {
8      for (auto j = 0; j < t.size() + 1; ++j) {
9        if (i == 0) memo[i][j] = j;
10       else if (j == 0) memo[i][j] = i;
11       else {
12         auto deletion = 1 + memo[i-1][j];
13         auto insertion = 1 + memo[i][j-1];
14         auto substitution =
15           memo[i-1][j-1] +
16           ((s[i-1] == t[j-1]) ? 0 : 1);
17         auto transoposition =
18           (i > 1 && j > 1 && s[i-1] == t[j-2] &&
19            s[i-2] == t[j-1]) ?
20             1 + memo[i-2][j-2] :
21             std::numeric_limits<int>::max();
22         memo[i][j] =
23           std::min(deletion,
24           std::min(insertion,
25           std::min(substitution,
26                    transoposition)));
27       }
28     }
29   }
30   return memo[s.size()][t.size()];
31 }
```

The algorithm above is quadratic since every entry of the matrix is calculated prior to the Damerau-Levenshtein distance known.

There are many other useful modifications to the calculation of edit distance. For instance, each of the operations can be given an independent weight in order to bias towards or against certain types of operations. Sequence alignment and string similarity are also problems equivalent to edit distance. Notably, the Smith-

Waterman sequence alignment gives a single weight to the operations of Levenshtein distance in order to determine a similarity score between two strings.

14.4 Equal partition knapsack problem

In the previous sections, we have looked at problems solved by dynamic programming that build up solutions from sub-arrays of each parameter. In as much as there were two parameters, the sub problems were straightforward. In this section, we look at a problem in which the dynamic programming solution works with sub problems that are not immediately obvious, and whose solution is not quadratic.

In the partition problem we are given a sequence S of n elements that we want to partition into two subsequences A and B such that $\sum_A = \sum_B$. As it is not always possible to find such a separation, we instead look for the partition A and B that minimizes the difference of the sum $|\sum_A - \sum_B|$. In addition, to simplify matters we suppose that the elements of S are positive. We lose generality in this assumption as a constant can always be added to all elements of the sequence.

Let $\sum_S$ be the sum of all elements in S. Considering only two partitions, we know that $\sum_B = \sum_S - \sum_A$. The objective is minimized if we find A such that $\sum_A = \sum_S /2$. From this observation, we proceed to find such a subsequence A with this sum. Note that for each element $s \in S$ either $s \in A$ or $s \in B$. We look at constructing A from S to develop our sub problems.

Denote by S_i the sub-array $s_i, s_{i+1} \ldots, s_n$. For brevity, we denote by (k, S_i) the partition from the sub-array S_i with sum nearest k. We then have overlapping sub problems with optimal substructure defined as the following.

$$
(k, S_i) = \begin{cases} \emptyset & \text{if } k = 0, \\ \arg\min_{|k - \sum_X|} X \in \begin{cases} s_i \cup (k - s_i, S_{i+1}) \\ (k, S_{i+1}) \end{cases} & \text{otherwise} \end{cases}
$$

From the structure of these sub problems, the solution would be $O(k * n)$ if we can compute the difference in the sums of each partition in constant time. However, this difference is the sum of S minus the element.

To build a solution in a bottom up manner, we memoize the sum of subsequences. The vector `memo` contains the first subsequence of S found that sums to its index i. Note that as the values of S are non-negative, for every pair of values j and $\sum_S -j$ we need only store one subsequence. The other is the set complement. For completeness we store the redundant information at the cost of using extra space. A solution is provided in the following listing.

Listing 14.7: Equal Partition

```cpp
std::multiset<int> equal_partitions(
    const std::vector<int>& s) {
  auto sum = std::accumulate(s.begin(),
                             s.end(),
                             0);
  auto target = sum / 2;
  auto closest = sum;
  std::vector<std::multiset<int>> memo(sum + 1);
  memo[0] = {};
  memo[sum] =
    std::multiset<int>(s.begin(), s.end());
  for (auto i = 0; i < s.size(); ++i) {
    for (auto j = sum; j >= s[i]; --j) {
      if (memo[j].empty() &&
          (j == s[i] || !memo[j-s[i]].empty())) {
        memo[j] = memo[j-s[i]];
        memo[j].insert(s[i]);
        if (std::abs(target - closest) >
                std::abs(target - j)) {
          closest = j;
        }
      }
    }
  }
  return memo[closest];
}
```

The partition problem is a specialization of the knapsack problem. Since the knapsack problem is *NP*-complete, we can expect no better than a pseudo-polynomial solution.

Chapter 15

Enumeration

Enumeration is the act of generating all the elements of some collection.

We consider construction of three types of collections through enumeration; combinations, permutations, and partitions. A combination is a collection of sets of elements without order. A permutation is a set of elements that are distinct by their order. Moreover, a partition is a division of a set into distinct subgroups.

In this chapter, we look these common enumeration problems in detail. Our base set will be an alphabet of characters. We begin with the combinatorial task of enumerating all subsets of a set. We then discuss the permutation problem of generating all anagrams from a sentence. We consider next the problem of generating all partitions of a set, which then leads us to the problem of segmenting a string of characters into words.

15.1 Combinations

A common gating question is to enumerate the set of all subsets. To be more precise, from a set of given values S produce all possible subsets $\mathbb{P}(S)$. The larger set $\mathbb{P}(S)$ is called the power set of S. Note that the empty set is a subset of the power set.

Throughout this section and the next, we will use container classes, and our results are often container classes of container classes. To simplify the exposition, we use the following definitions here and throughout. The items are the units that compose sets, often characters.

Listing 15.1: Types for Enumerations

```
1  typedef int Item;
2  typedef std::set<Item> Combination;
3  typedef std::set<Combination> CombinationsSet;
```

We use set because order does not matter in combinations. To generate the power set, consider the basic cases. Suppose that $S = \{s\}$. Then the power set is the empty set $\emptyset$ and the set of only s. Now if we consider $S' = \{s, t\}$, then from $\mathbb{P}(S)$ we can construct $\mathbb{P}(S')$ if for every set in $\mathbb{P}(S)$ we add two sets to $\mathbb{P}(S')$. One set includes t and one set does not. Continuing in this way we recursively build the power set by first generating the power set of a subset and from that the larger power set.

Listing 15.2: Generate all Combinations

```
1  CombinationsSet powerset(std::set<Item> items) {
2    if (items.empty()) {
3      return {{}};
4    }
5    auto item = *items.begin();
6    items.erase(item);
7    auto subsets = powerset(items);
8    CombinationsSet retval(subsets);
9    for(auto subset : subsets) {
10     subset.insert(item);
11     retval.insert(subset);
12   }
13   return retval;
14 }
```

From the recursive definition, it is easy to see that the power set doubles with every additional element in S. Hence the size of the power set is $|\mathbb{P}(S)| = 2^{|S|}$. The total running time of `powerset` is exponential in the number of items.

Since exponential run time limits the utility of such an enumeration, we look for an iterative solution. To understand our solution, first consider any combination A in the power set. Notice that for each $s \in S$ either $s \in A$ or $s \notin A$. So if we put some order on the elements of S, the this inclusion or exclusion for A be expressed as a binary word. A value of 1 in position i means that i is in a set, and excluded otherwise. What we see is that every binary sequence from 0 to $2^{|S|} - 1$ corresponds to a member of the power set. This correspondence is the basis of an iterative solution.

Listing 15.3: Iteratively Generate all Combinations

```
1   CombinationsSet powerset(std::set<Item> s) {
2     if (s.empty()) {
3       return {{}};
4     }
5     std::vector<Item> indexed_set(s.begin(),
6                                   s.end());
7     CombinationsSet retval = {};
8     std::vector<bool> bitarry(s.size(), false);
9     Combination subset;
10    do {
11      subset = {};
12      for (size_t i = 0; i < s.size(); ++i) {
13        if (bitarry[i]) {
14          subset.insert(indexed_set[i]);
15        }
16      }
17      for (int i = 0; i < s.size(); ++i) {
18        bitarry[i] = bitarry[i] ? 0 : 1;
19        if (bitarry[i]) {
20          break;
21        }
22      }
23    } while (retval.insert(subset).second);
24    return retval;
25  }
```

Note that the only state needed to be stored between generation of combinations in the power set is the bit array and the order of enumeration of the underlying set. It is trivial to wrap this procedure in a class and thereby construct a generator for the power set. However, for simplicity all are enumerated above.

For me the iterative solution receives higher marks. The conceptual leap from seeing that the inclusion or exclusion character develops to the bijection between subsets and a binary representation is a sign of a good solution. The iterative solution is more efficient in its memory consumption and performance in practice. Further, it can be easily modified to a power set iterator without pre-computing the entire set by taking the counter as a state parameter.

15.2   Permutations

Permutations are re-arrangements of a set or items. The following type definitions clarify this difference between a permutation and a combination.

Listing 15.4: Types for Permutations

```
1  typedef std::vector<Item> Permutation;
2  typedef std::set<Permutation> PermutationSet;
```

Each permutation in the permutation set contains every item in the base set. The only difference is the order in which the items appear. It is easy to see that there are $n!$ permutations for a set S of size n. There are n choices for the first element. Once a choice is made, there are then $n-1$ choices for the second, $n-2$ choices for the third and so on until we are left with a single choice for the last item.

This descriptive construction of a permutation leads directly to a recursive solution to the problem of enumerating permutations.

```
   Listing 15.5: Generate all Permutations

1  PermutationSet permutations(
2      const std::set<Item>& items) {
3      PermutationSet retval;
4      std::function<void(std::vector<Item>,
5                         Permutation*)>
6      recursive_call = [&recursive_call, &retval] (
7          std::vector<Item> items,
8          Permutation* current) {
9          if (items.empty() && !current->empty()) {
10             retval.insert(*current);
11             return;
12         }
13         for (auto i = 0; i < items.size(); ++i) {
14             auto item = items[i];
15             items.erase(items.begin() + i);
16             current->push_back(item);
17             recursive_call(items, current);
18             current->pop_back();
19             items.emplace(items.begin() + i, item);
20         }
21     };
22     std::vector<Item> indexed_items(items.begin(),
23                                     items.end());
24     Permutation current;
25     recursive_call(indexed_items, &current);
26     return retval;
27 }
```

Developing an iterative enumeration is more delicate for permutations than for combinations. Unlike with combinations, there is no bijection from Boolean arrays to elements of the permutation set. However, a solution can be constructed.

To begin we track the state of construction of a partial solution in the recursive solution. The recursive solution proceeds from an empty permutation to a complete permutation in the forward direction. From a partially constructed permutation consisting of the prefix, the next value chosen must be an element that does not yet exist in the permutation. The choice is made, the partial solution updated, and the next level of recursion will then have fewer choices.

Once a permutation is complete, it is stored and the recursion backtracks disassembling the permutation and tracking what values are left to choose. This is done by marking the used element. The solution here uses a modified breadth first search.

So we have two states, forward and backward. The forward state choses an item from those not yet used, and builds up a partial solution. The backward state disassembles a partial solution until a point a value is found that has not yet been used at a location in the partial solution. At that time, we move forward again. The following listing converts this description into a procedure.

Listing 15.6: Iteratively Generate all Permutations

```
1  PermutationSet permutations(
2      const std::set<Item>& items) {
3      if (items.empty()) return {};
4      PermutationSet retval;
5      Permutation permutation(items.size(), -1);
6      std::set<Item> available(items);
7      std::vector<std::set<Item>> remaining(
8          items.size());
9      remaining[0] = available;
10     size_t index = 0;
11     bool build_forward = true;
12     while (!remaining[0].empty()) {
13       if (build_forward) {
14         auto item = *remaining[index].begin();
15         permutation[index] = item;
16         available.erase(item);
17         if (available.empty()) {
18           retval.insert(permutation);
19           build_forward = false;
20           continue;
21         }
22         remaining[++index] = available;
23         continue;
24       }
25       while (!build_forward) {
26         remaining[index].erase(permutation[index]);
27         available.insert(permutation[index]);
28         permutation[index] = -1;
29         if (!remaining[index].empty() || !index) {
30           build_forward = true;
31           continue;
32         }
33         --index;
34       }
35     }
36     return retval;
37  }
```

For permutations, the recursive solution is much cleaner and simpler to follow. However, it is true that the state required to convert the iterative solution to a generator is still small. From studying the code, it is simply what has been used and what is still available to be used. Moreover, when dealing with the possibility of extremely large permutation sets, some leeway must be made for complexity.

15.3   Partitions

A partition is a division of a set into disjoint, non-empty subsets. Similar to a combination, the order of the elements within the subsets does not matter. However, a partition differs from a combination in two ways. First, every item of the set must be in some subset of the partition. Second, the number of subsets can vary.

Since the number of subsets varies, the number of partitions of a finite set is very large. Consider a set S of size n. Bell's number, B_n, is the number of partitions of S. Since there is at most 1 set if $n = 1$, $B_1 = 1$. If we add another element s to S, then we construct new partitions in two ways. First, we simply add the single element subset $\{s\}$ to every partition of S. Second given a partition of S, for any distinct subset, we can construct a partition of $S + s$ by appending s to the subset. For each subset of size k we have n choose k possibilities. With the subset fixed we have B_{n-k} partitions in which that subset appears. Hence, we have the recursive formula.

$$B_{n+1} = \sum_{k=0}^{n} \binom{n}{n-k} B_{n-k} = \sum_{k=0}^{n} \binom{n}{k} B_k$$

From this description, we have a means to recursively construct partitions of a set. Using recursion we first generate all partitions of the subset without a single token. Then we make two passes for each partition in the result, and for each subset in the partition, we form a new partition by appending the token.

A partition is a set of sets. Then a declaration of a set of partitions is three sets in depth as it is all sets of sets of sets. For presentation we simplify this below.

Listing 15.7: Partition and PartitionSet Types

```
1 typedef std::set<std::set<Item>> Partition;
2 typedef std::set<Partition> PartitionSet;
```

The listing for partition generation follows.

Listing 15.8: Generate All Partitions

```cpp
PartitionSet partitions(
    const std::set<Item>& base_set) {
  std::function<
    void(std::set<Item>, PartitionSet*)>
      recursive_partitions =
        [&recursive_partitions]
          (std::set<Item> base_set,
            PartitionSet* current) {
      if (base_set.empty()) {
        return;
      }
      auto item = *base_set.begin();
      base_set.erase(item);
      PartitionSet retval;
      recursive_partitions(base_set, &retval);
      for(auto& partition : retval) {
        auto copy = partition;
        copy.insert({item});
        current->insert(copy);
        for (auto& subset : partition) {
          auto subset_copy = subset;
          subset_copy.insert(item);
          auto copy = partition;
          copy.erase(subset);
          copy.insert(subset_copy);
          current->insert(copy);
        }
      }
      if (retval.empty()) {
        current->insert({{item}});
      }
      return;
    };
  PartitionSet retval;
  recursive_partitions(base_set, &retval);
  return retval;
}
```

Note that in every iteration we take the following steps. First, we remove one item from the set, and we recurse to generate all partitions of the set of smaller size. In generating a solution, we add the single element set to each of the returning partitions. Finally, for each partition and for each subset, we form a new partition by adding the character to that subset.

As with permutation generation this implementation is not optimal. Instead of generating all partitions in a single pass, we could refactor the code to generate one partition per call. However, the listing reveals the iterative nature the recurrence relation of Bell's number.

15.4 Word segmentation

Word segmentation is an important problem in natural language programming. Languages such as Chinese, Japanese, and Korean are without word delimiters to aid in tokenization. At times, processed English text is provided as a stream of characters without spaces and word segmentation must be enacted.

Segmentation is the identification and separation of tokens from a sequence. Word segmentation is done by constructing the most likely partition of a string of characters into tokens

To measure the likelihood of segmentation, we suppose that we are given a dictionary `score_word` that provides the frequency of a word in the English language. We will take the frequency as a measure of the probability that a sequence of characters is a word. We then take the product of the probabilities of tokens as the likelihood of a particular segmentation.

As an example, consider the text `ISITI`. Two valid word splittings are `I SIT I` and `IS IT I`. To distinguish amongst them, the most likely is the one with maximum probability. Keep track of only the segmentation that gives the maximum.

$$\Pr(\texttt{I SIT I}) = \Pr(\texttt{I})\Pr(\texttt{SIT})\Pr(\texttt{I})$$
$$\Pr(\texttt{IS IT I}) = \Pr(\texttt{IS})\Pr(\texttt{IT})\Pr(\texttt{I})$$

A naive attempt at word segmentation would be to score all partitions. However as we have seen the possible number of segmentations grows exponentially as this is a partition problem.

To get around this we use memoization. The approach is to memoize the most likely segmentation of prefixes of the token string. In the listing below, we memoize to map called `memo`. This data structure is indexed by prefix length. For each prefix of length k

the memo stores both the best found prefix segmentation and the
likelihood of that segmentation.

```
Listing 15.9: Word Segmentation
1  Segmentation segment_word(
2      const std::string& tokens) {
3    std::unordered_map<
4      size_t, std::tuple<Segmentation, double>>
5        memo = {{0,
6                  make_tuple(Segmentation(), 1.0)}};
7    for (auto i = 1; i <= tokens.length(); ++i) {
8      for (auto j = 0; j < i; ++j) {
9        auto suffix = tokens.substr(j, i-j);
10       auto entry = score_word.find(suffix);
11       auto score = 0.0;
12       if (entry != score_word.end()) {
13         score = score_word[suffix] *
14                   std::get<1>(memo[j]);
15       }
16       if (memo.end() == memo.find(i) ||
17           score >= std::get<1>(memo[i])) {
18         memo[i] =
19           std::make_tuple(std::get<0>(memo[j]),
20                           score);
21         std::get<0>(memo[i]).push_back(suffix);
22       }
23     }
24   }
25   return std::get<0>(memo[tokens.length()]);
26 }
```

In the listing above we have used the data type Segmentation.

```
Listing 15.10: Segmentation Data Type
1  typedef std::vector<std::string> Segmentation;
```

The above word segmentation has decent efficiency when compared again enumerating all permutations. For every character, all

possible suffix strings ending in that character are scored. As such, we have a quadratic algorithmic.

Chapter 16

Probability

Programming problems often test a candidate's ability to understand and use randomization.

The simplest questions ask to write a function that produces a random telephone number or deal a hand from a deck of cards. These questions require only careful tracking of the state space and use of the random functions provided from the standard library.

There are two common advanced questions that are also asked, and often formal proofs of their effectiveness are required of a candidate to test understanding. The first is shuffling a deck of cards to produce a random sequence. The second is sampling uniformly at random from a stream of integers. In this chapter, we look at solutions to both of these problems in detail.

However first we examine the pseudo-random generator available in the standard library and solve the basic question of how to deal a hand from a deck of cards.

16.1   Random Number Generation

Prior to support for C++11, the standard only supported the rand api. This library function used the machine's native source of randomness to produce a pseudo-random sequence of bits uniformly from the range of 0 to RAND_MAX, where RAND_MAX is a constant provided in cstdlib.h. Many implementations produced only 15 bits of randomness, and the pseudo-random value had to be cast or converted to the proper output.

The new standard supports generating pseudo-random values through apis such as uniform_int_distribution and normal_distribution defined in the random library. To use one of the sampling functions a random device is required. This defines the source of randomness, be it a local file or an algorithm. The device is then used by a pseudo-random number generator algorithm that is declared by the user. The sampling api uses the generator to produce pseudo random values. Support in C++11 is much richer than the former standard libraries, natively supporting more distributions than the uniform distribution.

In the following we will make use of uniform_int_distribution frequently. We use a global variable declared as rng defined using the Mersenne twister generator declared in the listing below.

Listing 16.1: Random Device mt19937

```
1 #include <random>
2 std::random_device rd;
3 std::mt19937 rng(rd());
```

The rng object defined above is a pseudo-random number generating algorithm. The rd object is a random device, it provides access to a machine's native source of randomness.

16.2   Dealing from a deck of cards

We first consider the programming problem of dealing a hand from a deck of cards. We model the deck as a vector of integers. We choose hand_size elements from the array at random, and return them in the container provided by the caller.

A solution is given in the listing below.

Listing 16.2: Deal a Hand

```
1  void deal(std::vector<int> deck,
2             size_t hand_size,
3             std::vector<int>* hand) {
4    for (int i = 0; i < hand_size; ++i) {
5      std::uniform_int_distribution<unsigned> dist(
6          0,
7          deck.size() - 1);
8      auto index = dist(rng);
9      hand->push_back(deck[index]);
10     deck.erase(deck.begin() + index);
11   }
12 }
```

Notice we invoke the copy constructor when passing the deck to the function. This is done since the algorithm requires we modify the deck to avoid choosing duplicates. This can be avoided by regenerating a different index if a collision is detected, but this process is more straightforward.

16.3 Shuffling a deck of cards

Our next programming problem is shuffling a deck of cards. A standard deck of cards is again modeled as 52 integers stored in an integer array.

We consider two shuffling algorithms as solutions to this problem. The first, called the Riffle Shuffle, attempts to model human shuffling. The second is called Selection Shuffle. It is an optimized shuffle. We formally prove that it provides a uniform sample from the set of ordered decks. Both are interesting in their own right, and either provides a provably random shuffle. However, they have different uses.

16.3.1 Riffle shuffle

A routine shuffle of a deck of cards is the composition of a riffle and a cut. A riffle is the action of choosing a pivot element, dividing the deck into two partitions at the pivot, and then merging the deck by interleaving the partitions. A cut is choosing another pivot, and swapping the order of the two partitions defined by this pivot. To achieve a uniform distribution of the cards independent of the starting position, this process needs to be repeated some number of iterations. The number is a function of the size of the deck. Concretely, for a standard 52 card deck seven Riffle shuffles are necessary to achieve a sample from the uniform distribution.

The following listing is a translation of these actions into code. The shuffle method takes as input the number of iterations of the riffle shuffle and a deck of cards.

Listing 16.3: Riffle Shuffle

```
 1  void shuffle (size_t num, std::vector<int>* deck) {
 2    std::uniform_int_distribution<int> dist(
 3        0,
 4        deck->size() - 1);
 5    while (num-- > 0 && deck->size()) {
 6      std::vector<int> temp(deck->size());
 7      auto pivot = dist(rng);
 8      int i;
 9      for (i = 0;
10          i < pivot && (i + pivot) < deck->size();
11          ++i) {
12        temp[2 * i] = (*deck)[i];
13        temp[2 * i + 1] = (*deck)[pivot + i];
14      }
15      for (auto j = 0; j + i < pivot; ++j) {
16        temp[2 * i + j] = (*deck)[j + i];
17      }
18      for (auto j = 0;
19          (j + i + pivot) < deck->size();
20          ++j) {
21        temp[2 * i + j] = (*deck)[pivot + i + j];
22      }
23      deck->assign(temp.begin(), temp.end());
24      std::rotate(deck->begin(),
25                  deck->begin() + dist(rng),
26                  deck->end());
27    }
28  }
```

The algorithm is linear in time and space. However, notice that every iteration writes every element twice. Further, interleaving requires temporary storage equal to the size of the initial array. We also require a number of passes specified to get a random shuffle. All of these drawbacks can be removed in an optimized algorithm.

16.3.2 Selection shuffle

In selection shuffle, we maintain the linear run time but remove the necessity of extra storage and multiple writes. This is done by first considering that no index in the deck is fixed. We then select an element uniformly at random from the deck, and by moving it to the lowest unset index in the deck fix its position in the output. We continue to iterate over the unchosen elements until we have fixed all locations in the deck.

Listing 16.4: Selection Shuffle

```
1  void shuffle (std::vector<int>* deck) {
2    for (int i = deck->size(); i > 0; --i) {
3      std::uniform_int_distribution<int> dist(
4          0,
5          i - 1);
6      auto choice = dist(rng);
7      std::swap((*deck)[i-1], (*deck)[choice]);
8    }
9    return;
10  }
```

The algorithm is straightforward, and much simpler than riffle shuffle in both code complexity and time complexity.

To prove correctness, we need to calculate the probability the element m is assigned to the ith index. To do so, let's first consider the probability that element m appears at the last index. This is $1/n$, as the last index is chosen only in the first iteration and every element has equal probability of being chosen. To calculate the probability the m is in index $i \neq n$, we note that it cannot have been assigned to any larger index n to $i + 1$. Each iteration choses uniformly from the previously unassigned values, hence the probability that m has not been assigned is

$$Pr(m \text{ not in } n,\ldots,i+1) = Pr(m \text{ not in } n)\cdots Pr(m \text{ not in } i+i)$$
$$= \frac{n-1}{n}\cdots\frac{i+2}{i+1}$$

Similarly, the probability that m is assigned to index i given that it is available is $1/i$. Writing out the full product, we see that the adjacent numerators and denominators cancel leaving us with our desired value.

$$Pr(m \text{ assigned to index } i) = Pr(m \text{ not in } n,\cdots,i+1)\cdot\frac{1}{i}$$
$$= \frac{n-1}{n}\cdot\frac{n-2}{n-1}\cdots\frac{i}{i+1}\cdot\frac{1}{i}$$
$$= \frac{1}{n}$$

16.4   Sampling from a stream

The second problem of this chapter comes from the field of online algorithms. The input is dynamic and is not available for multiple reads in these problems. Further, the point of termination is not known before hand. Suppose you are given a stream of integers. It is not known ahead of time how many elements are in the stream. The problem is to write an algorithm for which samples uniformly when the stream terminates.

16.4.1   Sampling a single element

The solution requires that the probability with which we choose and element change with the number of elements we see. If there is but a single element, we must always choose it. If there is a second element, we must choose it with probability of $1/2$. By doing so, we over-write the first element with probability $1/2$. At the point when we see the nth element, we want to chose that element with probability of $1/n$. We return the chosen element when we no longer have an option to choose an element.

```
Listing 16.5: Uniform Random Sample
1  int select(std::istream& stream) {
2    int choice = 0;
3    int sample;
4    int count = 0;
5    while (stream >> sample) {
6      count++;
7      std::uniform_int_distribution<int> dist(
8          0,
9          count - 1);
10     if (0 == dist(rng)) {
11       choice = sample;
12     }
13   }
14   return choice;
15 }
```

To prove correctness of the algorithm, we use induction on the number of elements. As noted, if the stream consists of a single element, the algorithm returns the first and only element. Hence, the algorithm is correct for $n = 1$. Now suppose that the algorithm samples uniformly from the first $n-1$ elements. Consider its actions when provided with the next element. The probability that the last element is chosen is $1/n$, so the probability that it is not chosen is $1-1/n = (n-1)/n$. Hence the probability that element m for $m < n$ chosen by the algorithm is the probability that m was chosen when it was first encountered and no other element was chosen afterward. Since each choice of elements after m is independent of all others, we have the following result after the product telescopes.

$$
\begin{aligned}
Pr(m) &= \frac{1}{m} \cdot \frac{(m+1)-1}{m+1} \cdot \frac{(m+2)-1}{m+2} \cdots \frac{(n-1)-1}{n-1} \frac{n-1}{n} \\
&= \frac{1}{m} \cdot \frac{m}{m+1} \cdot \frac{m+1}{m+2} \cdots \frac{n-2}{n-1} \frac{n-1}{n} \\
&= \frac{1}{n}
\end{aligned}
$$

Hence the probability that any element m is chosen is $1/n$, the uniform distribution.

16.4.2   Sampling n elements

A straightforward generalization of the previous question is often asked as a follow up. The question is modified to require that algorithm produces a random sample of m elements from the stream. The idea is to choose as above, modifying the selection criteria so that we have m/n chance of choosing the next element in the stream. If we do choose to keep the element, we need to evacuate a single random element from those that we have previously chosen. Translating this algorithm into C/C++, we have.

Listing 16.6: Uniform Random Sample of m Elements

```cpp
std::vector<int> select(std::istream& stream,
                        size_t m) {
   std::vector<int> arr(m);
   int count = 0;
   int sample;
   while (stream >> sample) {
     count++;
     if (count <= m) {
       arr[count - 1] = sample;
       continue;
     }
     std::uniform_int_distribution<int> dist(
         0,
         count - 1);
     if (m > dist(rng)) {
       std::uniform_int_distribution<int> dist(1,m);
       arr[dist(rng)-1] = sample;
     }
   }
}
```

The proof of correctness of this algorithm is similar to the proof above. For the element n, it is clearly chosen with probability m/n at discovery. For any element $k < n$, it is initially chosen with probability m/k. It can only be evacuated if either a successor element is not chosen or in the event one is chosen it is not evacuated in the insertion. For element $k + i$, k remains with probability

$$(1-\frac{m}{k+i})+\frac{m}{k+i}(1-\frac{1}{m}) = \frac{k+i-m}{k+i}+\frac{(m-1)(k+i)}{m} = \frac{k+i-1}{k+i}$$

From this, we can calculate that the probability that the kth element is chosen is after n elements are seen is

$$\begin{aligned} Pr(m) &= \frac{m}{k} \cdot \frac{k}{k+1} \cdot \frac{k+1}{k+2} \cdots \frac{n-1}{n} \\ &= \frac{m}{n} \end{aligned}$$

Where again the product telescopes. Since every element has the same probability of being chosen, we have shown that the choice is uniform. We have proven that the algorithm samples uniformly at random.

Afterward

With that, we complete this step in our journey through this set of advanced algorithms. I hope you've enjoyed the problem choice and the style the solutions have taken. We've covered a lot of material and studied some difficult algorithms. I enjoyed the process of writing this book, and sincerely hope you enjoyed reading it.

At this ending, I feel the journey is somewhat incomplete. There are areas of both programming and the technical interview that I have not addressed but which are fascinating. Three such areas are systems programming, design problems, and Fermi problems.

There are three systems programming problems that I think every engineer should be able to solve. These are the problems of writing an operator new, designing a thread pool, and implementing a simple socket based client-server application. These problems benefit from the concurrency and thread apis of C++11. However, their discussion is out of place in a text focused specifically on algorithms.

Design problems are extremely engaging, but they are best presented with diagrams and flow charts instead of code listings. The most interesting design problems I have recently encountered are building a web crawler, designing an internet scale archival system, and designing a url shortening web service. It is worth everyone's time to sit down and work through two or three designs for these systems. In my experience, engineers rarely come up with the same design.

Fermi problems are estimation tasks that require little more than extrapolation from simple observations. The most commonly asked Fermi problems are how many piano tuners are in San Francisco or how many man holes are in Seattle. To approach the first estimate the population a single piano tuner can serve, and suppose that the city is in economic equilibrium. For the second, estimate the number of covers in a square block, and extrapolate to the geographic area of the region. While the solutions are not unique, the approach that is being tested when these questions are asked.

Perhaps in another volume, until then I lay this work aside.

Index

www.ingramcontent.com/pod-product-compliance
Lightning Source LLC
Chambersburg PA
CBHW051237050326
40689CB00007B/951